T3-BOR-574

Contents at a Glance

The Computer Virus
Protection Handbook

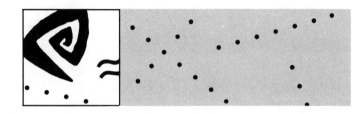

The Computer Virus
Protection Handbook

Colin Haynes

SYBEX®

San Francisco • Paris • Düsseldorf • Soest

Acquisitions Editor: Dianne King
Developmental Editor: Cheryl Holzaepfel
Copy Editor: Ami Knox
Technical Editor: D. Andrew Tauber
Word Processor: Deborah Maizels
Book Designer and Chapter Art: Suzanne Albertson
Technical Art: Jeffrey James Giese
Desktop Publishing Operator: Bob Myren
Production Editor: Carolina L. Montilla
Indexer: T.G. McFadden
Cover Designer: Thomas Ingalls + Associates
Cover Photographer: David Bishop

Library of Congress Card Number: 90-70167
ISBN: 0-89588-696-0
Manufactured in the United States of America
10 9 8 7 6 5 4 3 2 1

This book is dedicated to those hackers who, through their initiative, creativity, technical prowess, and integrity, will continue to advance the positive aspects of computing while helping to protect all of us who use computers against viruses and other electronic evils.

In particular, it pays tribute to John McAfee and other software engineers, researchers, and computing enthusiasts who defied ill-informed criticism and commercial pressures to sound unpopular early warnings of the dangers viruses present to a society increasingly dependent on smart machines that may no longer always obey us.

The nation's 50 million personal computers will remain highly vulnerable to attack by "worms" and "viruses." Indeed, they will likely become more susceptible, thanks to the increased inter-connection of PCs, the often lengthy "incubation" time required for viruses to be widely disseminated, the "time-bomb" delays written into some versions and the growing ease of copying or modifying viral codes.

Moreover, because so many critical aspects of modern life depend on computer programs—engineering design, medical diagnosis, safety control, financial systems, etc.—the destructive potential is greater every year... Some of the new (viruses and worms) will be especially damaging if they get into core data-banks of networks, where the information wealth of our society increasingly resides... Computerized information is all too mortal.

—David Stang, Director of Research for the National Computer Security Association, writing in the *Washington Post*, January 1990

Acknowledgments

My thanks to Cheryl Holzaepfel, Ami Knox, Dan Tauber, and their colleagues at SYBEX, and to my agent Bill Gladstone for bringing me together with a publishing team that really cares about accuracy and authors. Cheryl's tolerance, encouragement, and professionalism are models of excellence in editing.

Kate Drew-Wilkinson has, as always, been inspiring and supportive, while John McAfee and Joe Hirst have been generous guides on this, my second voyage into the mysteries of the computer virus phenomenon. Michael Alexander's generosity and integrity during the establishment of the International Computer Virus Institute were invaluable in making the completion of this book possible.

Special thanks to two of my neighbors in the Sausalito houseboat community, Ted Nelson and Norman Carlin, and to Presidents Ronald Reagan and George Bush. Ted, that distinguished guru of hypertext, has shared his unique perspectives of the passions and the potential of computing. Norman, a plumber who cares, bought his first computer while I was working on this manuscript. His cheerful interruptions with questions as he battled with the hardware and software were welcome reminders that the technology is still not sufficiently accessible to all of us who can use and enjoy it. Both influenced, more than I realized at the time, the style and content of this book. The actions and words of Ronnie and George gave me valuable leads to the powerful human forces involved in the computer virus phenomenon. They showed me that there may be no rational explanation as to why both leaders and followers damage their own societies. Also, by following American politics and business more closely, I acquired a better understanding of the motivations of maverick hackers. I cannot agree with extreme tactics that include deploying damaging viruses, but I acknowledge that many hackers feel passionately about the dangers of their technology enhancing the power of governments, corporations, and individuals with questionable ethical values.

Table of Contents

Introduction

Malicious software vandals are trying to take control of your computer. This book warns you about the methods and weapons they are using to attack your system and tells you how to protect your data and fight back.

The Computer Virus Protection Handbook is the equivalent of an intensive emergency planning seminar. It contains the essential information that anyone who uses computers or manages an enterprise dependent on electronic data processing needs to know about computer viruses. Included with the book is a disk containing two programs important to understanding and coping with the virus epidemic. ViruScan is one of the most effective antiviral software programs available. Use it to protect your system immediately, and follow the instructions on keeping it up to date as new diagnostic and defensive techniques evolve to keep pace with new strains of viruses. The second program is actually a collection of programs called the Virus Simulation Suite. Only when you see a virus attack in progress can you start to relate to the problem in perspective. These virus simulation programs provide the experience of a virus infection in a form that does not endanger your data or your system.

Every system is at risk from a virus attack. Read on and you will be able to ascertain your degree of exposure, and how to reduce it substantially. You will learn what malicious software is, why it is being created, and how it penetrates innocent systems. Then you will acquire the knowledge to defend your computer against attack. Much of this advice can help with other data processing emergencies also—from earthquakes to spilled coffee.

Understanding the information in this book does not require any special technical knowledge. The subject matter is fascinating in its own right, so whether you are a corporate manager or an individual user, you will be entertained as well as informed as you read through the chapters.

If you are concerned about protecting a business or other organization from viruses, the information in this book can be a resource for motivating and informing staff and colleagues. It could, for example, form the basis for an in-house computer virus hot line customized to fit individual corporate requirements. A virus hot line and a user support service for applications programs such as word processing or databases might be combined. This can be particularly appropriate when staff change frequently, or when program upgrades occur and there is an ongoing training requirement. This book can also provide course material for any organization to stage its own internal seminars and training programs.

≈ The Dangers Are Real

Computer viruses are a very real danger to the well-being of our society—both the government and the business community now belatedly acknowledge the realities of the epidemic. In its special publication, "Computer Viruses and Related Threats: A Management Guide," the Department of Commerce's National Institute of Standards and Technology warns, "The damage can vary widely, and can be so extensive as to require the complete rebuilding of all system software and data. Because viruses can spread rapidly to other programs and systems, the damage can multiply geometrically."

The respected information systems management journal *Computerworld* compared the vulnerability of both government and corporate systems to oil tankers threatening at any time to run aground and cause a disaster with frightening consequences. In the article "Lax security invites liability nightmare" *Computerworld* warned in its March 26, 1990, issue that information systems managers might soon find themselves hauled into court, as was the captain of the Exxon Valdez, on criminal charges. In their case, it would be "failure to adequately protect their corporate computer systems against hacker attacks, viruses and other serious breaches of security."

Some experts rank the risk so highly that they believe if executives understood the magnitude of their exposure to the loss of vital data, and to possible liability suits, they might close down their networks immediately.

If you have not yet had direct personal experience of a computer virus infection, the statistical reality of the geometric growth of the infection rate means that you probably will quite soon. The sheer volume of the over 80 viral strains that are now in circulation means that the risks to systems, particularly those linked to each other over networks, must escalate further.

So it is vital that both individuals and organizations to whom computing is important adopt a comprehensive and coordinated policy to defend their systems against virus infection and acquire the capacity to take effective action should an infection occur.

≈ You Don't Need to Be an Expert to Protect Your System

You do not need to be a computer expert to understand this book and acquire the knowledge to keep control of your computing. Indeed, this book is intended to reinforce your fundamental right *not* to be obliged to study how a computer and its programs work to be able to take advantage of this wonderful technology.

Most of us do not want to be hackers or programmers. We simply want computers to work for us just as we expect our automobiles, refrigerators, and television sets to function without requiring us to be experts in their engineering. But the machines that help us manage information do demand a more intimate and complex relationship. We cannot completely distance ourselves from a basic understanding of how they function and why they may malfunction.

But once you have read the early chapters describing the basics of how viruses are created and spread, you will be empowered to choose a defensive strategy based on your particular needs. You may decide to do nothing and accept a calculated risk. That is your right, but I hope that you will come to the conclusion that the precautions to reduce that risk to minimal proportions are so undemanding that they are very worthwhile. In fact, with very little effort, you can reduce your risk of infection by 95 percent or more, and enhance the prospects for recovering lost data if you do become a victim. It's well worth finding out these facts. They are brought together in this book so that, after just a few hours, you will know all you really *need* to know about computer viruses.

≈ A Brief Tour Through the Chapters

The first few chapters of *The Computer Virus Protection Handbook* familiarize you with the virus epidemic. You will learn about the extent of the problem, how viruses affect a computer system, and get answers to some of the common questions about viruses.

Chapter 4 explains how to use the Virus Simulation Suite programs that are included on the disk that accompanies this book. These programs safely simulate the actions of several common computer viruses so you'll know how an infection may manifest itself if you should become the target of an attack.

However, as Chapter 5 explains, your computer may behave strangely for reasons other than a virus infection. Many symptoms of a virus attack are similar to the symptoms of hardware or software problems—this chapter gives you tips on how to tell the difference.

If you contract a virus, Chapter 6 will lead you through the crisis step by step. By following the procedures in this chapter, you will be able to act swiftly and intelligently to minimize the damage from a virus attack.

Of course, the best strategy is prevention. Chapter 7 gives you practical advice about protecting your data, including a close look at some dangerous computing habits that may open doors to a virus attack or other computer trouble.

Chapter 8 introduces you to the villains of the virus epidemic. Here you will learn about the characteristics of Disk Killer, Dark Avenger, the Jerusalem, the now-famous Columbus Day virus, and more.

In Chapter 9 you will take a look at how the computer virus epidemic could change the way we compute in the future.

If you don't have a disaster plan ready (and you should) in case of a virus attack, or even natural disasters, Chapter 10 will show you how. You will learn how to determine what data is really vital, how to protect it in a crisis, and how to restore your data processing operations with minimum disruption.

Chapter 11 explains how to use the other program on the disk that accompanies this book—ViruScan. ViruScan is an easy-to-use antiviral software program that will check out your system for viruses and in many cases tell you how to eradicate them. Unlike many other antiviral programs, ViruScan's usefulness never becomes outdated because you can easily obtain updated versions of the program as information becomes available about new and modified viruses. ViruScan's proven track record makes it one of the most effective and reliable antiviral programs available.

The information printed in this book, plus the simulations and the protection software contained on the disk, form a comprehensive survival kit to help you through the computer virus epidemic. It has been a theme of the Information Revolution that knowledge is power. In this book is the knowledge that will help to provide you with the power to combat the virus threat to your system.

CHAPTER

1

Computer Viruses—an International Menace

Many people still do not take computer viruses seriously. Ignorance is the main reason, closely followed by apathy and attitude. Some with commerical interests in the computer industry do not even want attention focused on this threat to our technological future and, apprehensive about negative publicity for their products and services, have done their best to discourage public debate of a phenomenon posing dangers to almost every activity in our contemporary, computer-dependent society.

Even many computer and security experts have been painfully slow to understand what viruses are, why they are created, and what dangers they pose. Computing expertise can actually get in the way of technical experts' initial understanding of this phenomenon because viruses are a concept that never used to figure at all in computer training or system design and operation. Computing and security in the pre-virus days had always been logical, factual activities where the gray areas of unpredictability present in such other fields as medicine had no place. That's why even experienced software engineers and security experts had difficulty relating to virus programs when they first became a problem.

During the Crimean War, the founder of modern nursing, Florence Nightingale, struggled to convince experienced military surgeons that their patients were dying in such large numbers because the surgeons did not disinfect their hands and their tools properly between operations, and so spread fatal infections. This classic example of the difficulties inherent in overcoming the set ideas of experts mirrors what is happening in the computer industry today.

It has taken too long to convince many computer experts of the need to keep their electronic tools clean. The Florence Nightingales of the computer world who voiced warnings of the dangers of viruses in the early days—people such as Professor Fred Cohen, who coined the name *computer virus* for self-replicating programs, and Silicon Valley software engineer

John McAfee, who founded the Computer Virus Industry Association (CVIA)—were greeted with skepticism by much of the computing establishment. Now if you read the enormous traffic on the CVIA bulletin board from virus victims, McAfee has become a hero to many for the warnings and the help he has given.

I received an initially negative reception also when, as a computer user and investigatory writer, I tried to spell out the dangers looming. The first book I tried to prepare on viruses in collaboration with an expert on computer security foundered because my coauthor would not believe that the disturbing predictions I was making were realistic. In fact, it is now difficult to exaggerate the potential harm that viruses have demonstrated they are capable of doing.

Even in late 1989, I was greeted with skepticism by most of the audience of executives at a computer industry conference when I said that many of their sales people were spreading virus infection by using their demonstration disks in potential customers' machines. Now, after some of their best corporate customers have suffered multiple infections as a result of such action, they are taking the epidemic seriously.

Most of the expert writers on computing whom we rely on to keep us abreast of important developments have done an inadequate job of covering the virus issue. Too often they have listened only to those with commercial interests who consistently played down the virus threat because of the damage it could do to sales.

By reading this book, you have indicated that you have a genuine desire to be briefed on this vital issue. In effect, you have taken the first step toward preventing your system and your data from joining the victims of virus infection. The vast majority of computers now face a substantial risk of contracting a computer virus at some time, but in the pages that follow you will learn how to recognize the danger signs and do something effective to prevent or at worst minimize the damage from an infection. This way you can protect your computer system and at the same time continue to enjoy the enormous assistance it provides, whether you are involved with large corporate systems or pecking your way hesitantly across the keyboard of your first personal computer.

≈ The Virus Problem Proliferates

The seventies saw the rapid development of the computer, the most significant new technology since the invention of the wheel. In the eighties the Information Age dawned and the power of electronic data processing was brought within the reach of ordinary people.

As we increasingly integrate this technology into our everyday lives, the nineties may prove to be the decade in which we battle to retain control of it. Our newfound power to process information and use machines in ways that enormously enhance the quality of our lives is under attack by vandals, pranksters, saboteurs, criminals, and social misfits.

Our newfound power to process information and use machines in ways that enormously enhance the quality of our lives is under attack .

The decade has started badly. As our political and business leaders slowly move to take action against the threat, computer virus infections have raced past the 2 million mark, according to CVIA estimates. New strains of malicious viruses able to pass from machine to machine, destroying and corrupting data, are being created and disseminated around the world. Our control over our computers has been challenged further by the emergence of viruses with the ability to mutate, thereby adapting themselves to almost any hostile environment, as do most biological viruses.

I have been accused of being sensationalistic and overly pessimistic about the potential harm that viruses can do. I encourage you to balance my views against not only those who seek to persuade you not to take viruses too seriously, but also the impartial, authoritative evidence of the danger of computer viruses in the public congressional records.

"The terrorists were in control of the airplane" was the analogy one witness used to describe a case presented to the U.S. Congressional House Judiciary Subcommittee on Computer Viruses, which began collecting evidence in 1989.

"The damage potential of viruses, as evidenced by recent cases, is overwhelming. The cost is staggering," the committee was told by Carolyn Conn, the expert witness representing the 10,000-member

Electronic Data Processing Auditors Association (EDPAA), an international group of computer security experts. At the congressional subcommittee hearing, Conn made this statement:

> *Viruses have cost corporations, government agencies, and educational institutions millions of dollars to prevent, detect, and recover from computer virus attacks. Viruses have the potential to destroy or disrupt computer systems and networks that provide vital communications and life support—for instance, local and long-distance telephone services; fire, police, and emergency services; military communications; financial transactions; and air traffic control.*

She emphasized that although viruses are attacking business, government, scientific, and academic sectors, it is impossible to accurately measure the extent of infection because so many corporate and government victims cover up attacks against themselves to conceal their vulnerability and avoid adverse publicity.

"It is evidently an issue that is underreported, probably rather dramatically," said subcommittee chairman Charles Schumer, a representative from New York, noting that even some of the systems of his fellow members of Congress had been infected. He tried hard to obtain accurate quantification of the extent of the problem, but the lack of reporting meant that only vague estimates of at least hundreds of thousands of infections were offered by the expert witnesses.

There is no dispute that the rate of infection is escalating—the EDPAA noted a tenfold increase in infections between the first and last two-month periods in 1988. Subsequently, the CVIA estimated that the infection rate increased again by a factor of at least ten during 1989, and will probably grow even faster in 1990.

The problem has even raised the moral issue of the individual's right to privacy versus the need to gather evidence to prove criminal activity. Gail Thackeray, an assistant district attorney from Arizona, explained to the congressional subcommittee that one of the legal anomalies benefiting computer vandals and obscuring the extent of the virus epidemic is the Electronic Communications Privacy Act. She could not conceal her frustration when she testified about how the corporate victims of virus infection would not provide the information necessary for the authorities to pursue the attackers.

"The Act stops us from getting the information to catch the villains," complained Thackeray to the legislators.

≈ Solving the Virus Problem —No Quick Fixes

An expert computer scientist, Professor Lance Hoffman of George Washington University, described the Internet network breakdown in which over 6,000 computers across America were disabled in October 1988 as the electronic data processing equivalent of the Three Mile Island incident. He warned the computer community to brace itself for the coming equivalent of the Chernobyl disaster.

"Our computer networks are now as vital to us as our national networks of highways and telephones," said Professor Hoffman. He warned that the proliferation of viruses might require regulation of the right to use those networks, just as the right to drive a vehicle is regulated. But he and the other experts who testified urged trying alternative measures before restricting the free flow of information to avoid clashing with fundamental First Amendment rights.

John Pickett, president of the Computer and Business Equipment Manufacturers Association—with members employing 1.5 million workers who produce nearly five percent of the gross national product—also warned Congress not to legislate against technology, but against those criminals abusing it. He told the subcommittee not to expect his members to come up with a "technological fix" to solve the virus problem.

"Each time we develop a new lock in the industry, someone eventually develops a pick that breaks it," Pickett explained.

The software side of the industry, represented by John Landry, chairman of the Virus Committee of the Computer Software and Services Industry Association, offered no quick fixes either.

"There are no silver bullets," he said.

Landry stressed the concern of both the industry and the legal profession that great care should be taken by legislators to define viruses accurately, distinguishing them from software bugs and other programming quirks. As an example, he cited a case in which a judge had declared that an access key (coding inserted in programs to prevent use by those who have not paid for the product) was legally a virus. The judge might have been challenged on the technical niceties of definition, but morally he could well have been on target, as this aggressive software-engineering device crashed a medical laboratory program. Such a decision indicates that using any kind of destructive programming to protect intellectual property rights in software, or as a means of forcing users to pay their bills to their suppliers or computer consultants, is no longer an acceptable practice.

Joseph Tompkins, chairman of the American Bar Association Task Force on Computer Crime, maintained that legal sanctions and law enforcement comprise only part of the solution to the virus problem (as is also the case in tackling another social ill, the use and distribution of illicit drugs). He pointed out the opportunities to amend existing legislation relating to trespass, computer crime, criminal negligence, fraud, and the like as possible alternatives to new laws.

Introducing civil law sanctions might help spread the prosecuting load on the assumption that if corporations can recover damages from virus attackers, they will be more motivated to pursue cases. But in reality, it is usually impossible to identify the creators of virus programs or those responsible for spreading them to particular systems, either deliberately or innocently. Most viruses are created secretly by individuals with no deep pockets to sue. It is predominantly a lonely activity carried out as a form of electronic vandalism, malicious amusement, revenge, or as a gesture of defiance against either a particular target or society as a whole.

The American computing community has received very little practical help from such government departments as the Federal Bureau of Investigation, the Defense Department, and the National Security Agency, although defending us against both domestic and foreign viruses is very much in the national interest.

Some of the experts who gave evidence to Congress think that virus research and defense are best entrusted to the people who really know about the technology, rather than to the government agencies. There was strong criticism of those computer security people who failed to learn from the UNIX system's vulnerability to infection, as demonstrated by the much publicized Internet infection. If Internet had been the learning experience it should have been, then a NASA system would not have been similarly compromised nearly a year later.

In another example, Marc Rottenberg, Director of Computer Professionals for Social Responsibility, described the mistake made by the Defense Department's Computer Emergency Defense Team. This virus SWAT squad advised users to combat a virus with a program that could have infected their systems!

≈ Taking the First Step toward Regaining Control of Your Computer

Tangible, disturbing evidence of the internationalization and organized spreading of virus infection presents itself at the start of the nineties decade. Thousands of medical and business professionals in many countries received a diskette through the mail that was labeled as containing information about AIDS. However, as soon as the diskette was inserted in a disk drive, it began destroying data.

The operation represented a very large investment in mailing lists, disk duplication, printing and postage costs, and the creation of phony front organizations. The perpetrators of this plot must have been extremely determined to cause a lot of damage to important data processing systems around the world if they were willing to go to such lengths to distribute this disk.

We can expect more remarkable examples of the lengths that individuals and groups will go to sabotage computers. This book will help you—and your organization, if you have responsibilities for managing data processing resources—to understand the threat and learn effective ways to combat it to retain control of your computers.

Viruses are cropping up everywhere and coming at us from all directions, as you will see in the following chapters. No software can be assumed to be completely inviolate, and that includes the hardwired programming in the chips that control your microwave and dishwasher; the automatic transmission, braking, and fuel injection systems in your car; the automatic pilot, air traffic control, and other computerized safety systems involved in air travel; and the computers that are used in our hospitals, emergency services, defense forces, and other vital aspects of contemporary society.

There is also a disturbing trend for viruses to be targeted at proprietary software, and some of the more sophisticated ones may avoid detection. Perhaps the perpetrators resent the high profits made by the big software companies, or feel that ideas and concepts that should be in the public domain are being hijacked for corporate gain.

Fortunately, virus infections are still the exception rather than the rule, but mathematical logic dictates that our exposure to risk will increase at a rapidly accelerating rate unless the majority of computer users take preventive actions. It is vital that both individuals and organizations to whom computing is important adopt comprehensive and coordinated policies to defend their systems against virus infection and take effective action should an infection occur.

This book is a practical tool to help formulate and implement those preventive and defensive measures. You do not need to be a computer expert to acquire the knowledge to keep control of your computer.

VIRUS FACT

Over 95 percent of all virus infections can be prevented by practicing simple, safe computing precautions.

Indeed, this book was written on the principle that you should *not* be obliged to study how a computer and its programs work in order to take advantage of this wonderful technology. Most of us do not want to be hackers or programmers. We only want computers to work for us just as we expect our automobiles, refrigerators, and television sets to function without requiring us to be experts in their electronic or engineering technicalities.

Unfortunately, computer viruses bring us up against the disturbing reality that machines can "disobey," not doing what we require of them because of errors either in the way that we build or use them. Viruses make what have become the most important devices in this phase of the Machine Age disturbingly unpredictable. Whether you rely on a computer to organize your thoughts into a great novel, to monitor the vital signs of the patient on whom you are performing triple bypass heart surgery, to maintain the accounts for your business, to transfer funds from one bank account to another, or to complete the connection when you telephone home, be warned: computers no longer perform a predictable, mechanized process likely to be disrupted only by mechanical malfunction or human error.

But don't lay the blame for viruses on the technology or the machines that execute that technology. The fundamental truth about computer viruses is that they are a people problem. People create viruses for various reasons. People disseminate virus infections either deliberately or as a result of the very human traits of innocence, ignorance, or carelessness. And the people who are the potential victims of this phenomenon can acquire the knowledge to turn a real threat into a reasonably calculated risk that they can live with.

Once you understand the basics of how viruses are created and spread, you are then empowered to choose a defensive strategy customized to your particular needs. You may decide to do nothing and trust to luck, or to the fact that your computing activities put you into a comparatively low-risk category. But before you make such a choice, be aware that the precautions to reduce the risk of having your computing disrupted by a viral infection are so undemanding that they are well worth the effort.

If you have not yet personally experienced a computer virus infection, the statistical reality of the exponential growth of the infection rate indicates that you probably will quite soon.

If you have not yet personally experienced a computer virus infection, the statistical reality of the exponential growth of the infection rate indicates that you probably will quite soon. The sheer volume alone of self-replicating viral strains that are now in circulation means that the risk of infection to systems, particularly those linked to each other over networks, will escalate further.

To prepare you for this challenging experience, the disk accompanying this book contains realistic simulations of attacks by some of the most common viruses. Don't be apprehensive about running them—they were created by Joe Hirst of the British Computer Virus Research Centre, one of the world's most renowned "good guys" in the virus war. He is much respected for his effort to protect organizations against infection.

We have tested the master disk with the other program that accompanies this book—the ViruScan antiviral software, which detects infections. So these programs, like most of the proprietary software that you now buy, have been well checked against contamination.

If you simply practice basic, safe computing principles, it will be unlikely that your system will become infected (just as safe sex dramatically reduces one's exposure to AIDS). If you go just one step further and use efficient virus prevention and detection software, the risk of your data being destroyed or compromised is further reduced substantially. Undertake the simple precautions required to facilitate recovery after an infection and you may never lose a byte of data during the virus epidemic.

In fact, with very little effort, your chances of infection can be reduced by 95 percent or more, and the prospects for recovery can also be increased. The facts that are brought together in this book should provide all you really need to know about computer viruses, and at the same time provide a few hours of what I hope will be entertaining reading.

CHAPTER

2

How a Virus Makes Your Computer Sick

How does a virus get into your computer and change its normal, healthy state into a form of electronic sickness? The process becomes more readily comprehended when compared to the way that the human body becomes sick when invaded by an infectious virus.

You use software to interact with your computer. Without software, the computer is just a useless machine. Software is both the medium through which we communicate instructions to the machine and the controlling mechanism that enables the machine to carry out those instructions correctly—the computer equivalent of the human brain and the central nervous system. Because a computer is a complex device capable of many different actions, the instructions to make it perform in the desired way tend to be complex also.

So to make computing easier and faster, we use two types of programs written by experts. The first is the *operating system*, the master program that controls all the basic computer functions. For example, it manages the way that the disk drives function (hence the acronym DOS for the most popular of such programs, the Disk Operating System). Macs, Amigas, minis, and mainframes all have operating system programs. Operating systems may be distinctive in their architecture, as the System and Toolbox combination for the Mac is radically different from DOS, but all perform similar functions. This means that all operating systems are vulnerable to computer viruses which, like biological viruses, are almost always "species specific." Just as pigs get swine fever but are not vulnerable to our own strains of influenza, Macs become infected with the MacMag virus, while IBM PCs and compatibles catch the Jerusalem virus.

There are only a few types of operating system programs, but there are many examples of the second type of software we use, the *application programs*. These work in conjunction with the operating system to carry out specific tasks, such as processing words, creating spreadsheets, playing games, or generating graphic designs.

If you are new to the concept of how computers function, think of a computer's *boot-up* procedure in terms of how you wake yourself up in the morning. Your body is the equivalent of the hardware in a computer system. While you were asleep, the brain and central nervous system fulfilled the role of a computer's operating system software, timing the heart to beat regularly to keep the blood coursing through the veins and arteries and monitoring and keeping under automatic control breathing and other vital functions.

When you activate your body from this state of rest, you give it instructions to apply itself to specific tasks—get out of bed, take a shower, make coffee, and drive to work. These voluntary commands, which you "load" into your brain, are the equivalent of computer application programs, which you load into your computer.

When your body is healthy, everything is controlled and predictable. You give your body instructions to apply itself to a particular task, and your arms, legs, hands, and eyes are coordinated by the brain and central nervous system to complete the task. If your body contracts an infection, both the "operating system" and "application programs" can malfunction. The brain has difficulty controlling the basic functions. You can try to command your body to perform certain tasks—to go jogging, for instance—but your head and limbs ache and you have no stamina. The infection prevents your body from completing the desired tasks.

A computer virus has similar effects on your computer. It can damage the operating system's ability to control basic functions, and when applications programs are run, it can override their activities also.

≈ How a Virus Enters Your System

While a virus is a software program with code that opens and closes electrical circuits within the computer, just like operating system and application programs, it has an important difference. Normal programs are your assistants. You buy them with the reasonable expectation that everyone involved in their creation and distribution are your allies in aiming for the same objective—to help you in your computing tasks.

Virus creators write programs with a completely different motivation. Because they may have a desire to cause trouble, they write programs that may harm instead of help you. Or they may create programs that carry unsolicited messages—an electronic form of junk mail or propaganda. As you do not need or want such software—and certainly would not knowingly buy it or even accept it as a gift—the creators must make these programs attractive or clever enough for you to allow them into your system.

One way is to disguise them so that they look like software designed to help you—a form of Trojan Horse. The harmful programs may be made to look like an interesting and useful program—perhaps a game or a time-saving applications program—in order to catch your attention. Such programs are often posted to a bulletin board, where they are then downloaded by users thinking they are receiving a fun or beneficial program.

VIRUS · FACT ·

Strange misbehavior by your computer is more likely to be caused by a software bug than it is by a virus. Check the README file in a new application program and call the supplier's support service to find out if your symptoms are bug, not virus, related.

Even that method is not very efficient, unless the harmful program is a computer virus. A virus relieves its creator of the task of spreading the aggressive program to many targets by reproducing and sending copies of itself out to penetrate other systems. This way the harmful action or message will spread quickly and extensively. Just one person

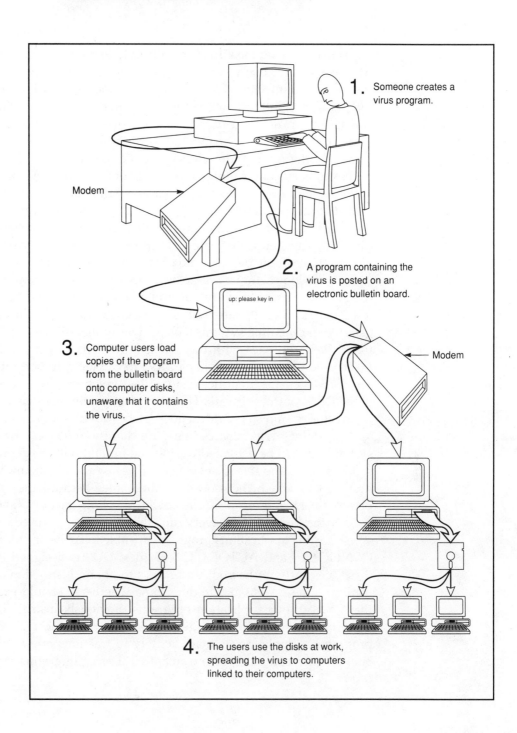

1. Someone creates a virus program.

Modem

2. A program containing the virus is posted on an electronic bulletin board.

up: please key in

3. Computer users load copies of the program from the bulletin board onto computer disks, unaware that it contains the virus.

Modem

4. The users use the disks at work, spreading the virus to computers linked to their computers.

needs to download the virus from the bulletin board for it to be well on its way to infecting many computer systems. Once into the downloader's system, it can infect the files on both hard and floppy disks. Then, when the first victim interacts with other computers over a network, or lends a contaminated disk to a friend, or loads one into a system at work, the virus may spread and have more opportunities to clone itself and do harm.

With the computer virus epidemic, we now are seeing thousands of computer systems running three types of programs—normal operating system programs, application programs deliberately installed and controlled by the user, and a virus program that is an unwelcome hidden interloper. Once inside a system, the virus intruder can behave in many different ways, either revealing its presence immediately or remaining hidden while doing damage and continuing to replicate.

It is logical for viruses to be designed to enter systems through the files they are most likely to encounter when they arrive. So the .COM, .EXE, or .SYS files that are part of every DOS system are the obvious targets. Other operating systems have similar vulnerabilities. The DOS command files (the ones with the extension .COM) and the .EXE files are executable programs that enable DOS to carry out important functions. The .SYS extension identifies system files, which are also an essential part of the DOS control software. There are also system files that are not listed in directories, and so provide a good place for viruses to hide.

Many *executable* files (meaning that these files can be run by the system) tend to be activated during the initial booting up procedure as soon as the computer is switched on. Consequently, many viruses are designed to attach themselves to these files because they are always present in DOS, they perform powerful, vital functions, and they are usually the first to be run every time the computer is started.

Many applications programs are able to create or modify existing CONFIG.SYS and AUTOEXEC.BAT files. DOS is designed to seek out these files early in the boot-up process to obtain instructions on how to configure the system and to determine whether it should execute a file that you or your application programs previously instructed it to run. Consequently, the virus can get an early start on most virus detection programs, completing its main activity in fractions of a second as you boot up your computer, before an antiviral program begins running.

≈ How a Virus Controls Your System

The most disturbing aspect of the virus epidemic is that average computer users are beginning to lose control of their computing environment. The orders that you, the computer user, give to the operating system and application programs can be overruled by a virus if it was programmed to do so. This takeover of control can be achieved in various ways once the virus is inside a system, depending on how the virus was programmed. Again, neither you nor your operating system and application programs have control over this, as the virus is not designed to play by your rulebook. It may act like the most contrary of children, doing the opposite of what you require. It can wreak mayhem among your files, destroying or altering them as it decides.

The key word in understanding how viruses function is *control*. The .COM and .EXE infector viruses interrupt normal computing activity at the first available opportunity to take control of the system while they copy themselves to new .COM and .EXE files.

They may attach to the file externally—as you would put a label on the outside of an ordinary paper file folder. Or they may find internal spaces that will accommodate the virus code within the coding for the program selected as a host. This is similar to concealing scraps of paper among the sheets of paper that are usually contained within a conventional file folder.

A virus can wreak mayhem among your files, destroying or altering them as it decides.

This process—interruption by the virus of normal computing activity, followed by the virus assuming control of the system to replicate and execute other tasks in its program, and then handing control back to the operating system and applications programs—can happen so quickly that the user is not aware that anything untoward has occurred.

Some of the .COM and .EXE infectors remain resident in the system's memory so that they can infect any program that is executed. They can modify the boot sector of a disk to make this a more comfortable environment for virus replication and other activity. They can also alter applications programs so that they are more accommodating to the needs of the virus.

A virus may seek out a system file that is already hidden, or change a file that it has infected into a hidden one that will not show up in directories.

A number of viruses hide in or alter for their own purposes the software that controls a system's internal clock. Often one of the first actions of a virus is to check the time and date in a system to see if these match the virus's programmed activation time. Another frequent first action by a virus is to check if there are any new files or disks accessible within the system for it to infect. If not, it may immediately pass control back to the operating system or application program and remain dormant until a suitable infection opportunity arises.

Much of the spread of viruses over networks and within organizations would be prevented if there was less exchange of executable code. For example, when a laser printer is shared by a number of system users, the disks used to print documents should contain only data.

Viruses may run concurrently with the operating system or application programs they have infected, carrying out their tasks either openly or hidden in the background. There are generic application infectors programmed to gain control of application programs when these are run, make whatever changes the virus has been instructed to do, then pass control back to the application. These viruses either hide in the application and take over some of its functions or, more frequently, attach themselves to the beginning or end of files. The programs that have been infected then become viruses themselves, spreading the infection and the harmful programming or message that the virus is carrying.

Some viruses will either assume control of the File Allocation Tables (FAT), which organize disk storage, or damage the FAT's ability to sort out where data is physically located on a disk. In effect, the virus either redraws the map of the disk or destroys it so that your operating system cannot find its way to any location on the disk where chunks of data have been saved.

The viruses that send clones of themselves into the RAM area, the main working memory of the computer, can stay concealed, ready to leap onto any receptive host that comes along, such as an uninfected diskette being loaded into one of the floppy drives. You might take a squeaky-clean diskette from its packaging and format it for the first time in drive A, and it immediately provides a host for a virus lurking in RAM, on the diskette in drive B, or on the hard disk. Viruses are like fleas waiting in the grass, ready to leap onto any dog that passes.

VIRUS FACT

Pirated programs are a major source of viruses. Never run a proprietary program that is not in its original sealed packaging without testing it first. Be particularly careful of shady dealers who offer to load the hard disk on your computer with "free" software. It is probably pirated software or public domain software and may be contaminated.

As we will see in the following chapters, once a virus has infected a system, it can prevent that system from operating as efficiently as normal, generate more severe symptoms of electronic illness, or cripple functions so that the system is no longer able to execute tasks. Some viruses effectively kill a system by destroying all the files it contains. Like some biological viruses, the symptoms may take considerable time to manifest themselves, so that before there are any tangible signs of trouble, the infection becomes well established, more widely spread, and consequently more difficult to eliminate.

The damage potential of a virus is not always in direct proportion to its complexity, size, or sophistication. A simple virus that quickly modifies the FAT, executes a hard-disk format command, or shuffles a few bytes of data in the root directory of a PC or into the Desktop file of a Macintosh can be fatal to your data processing activities. Even if the actual damage is small, the consequences may still be very serious. There are viruses that will merely change a byte of data here and there in a subtle, random manner that can go unnoticed for a very long time. This may not be too serious if the changes show up as apparent typing errors in a word processed document. The consequences could be far worse, though, if numerals are modified in accounting data or in the formulation of a pharmaceutical product.

> *Many routine computer malfunctions resemble viral symptoms; it is counterproductive to panic when the problem may be a software bug or a hardware malfunction.*

Your computer may become infected without displaying symptoms. In other words, your computer could be a virus carrier. We can expect this to happen increasingly as viruses are created for specific purposes and directed at particular targets, such as corporate or government systems. These viruses will find their way to the target by either passing through other systems or escaping into the general computing universe. If they include restrictive programming to prevent them from activating or doing damage unless they hit a specified target, then these viruses should not intentionally cause many problems to systems caught in their crossfire. However, many of these target-specific viruses could disrupt nontargeted computers with frenzied replicating activities. Or, if the virus contains programming bugs, it could turn into an unguided missile running out of control.

It is very easy to become a data processing hypochondriac. Many routine computer malfunctions resemble viral symptoms; it is counterproductive to panic when the problem may be a software bug or a hardware malfunction that is not going to spread, damage data, or require expensive expert assistance. These other causes of viral symptoms are discussed in detail in Chapter 5.

While safe computing practices are essential to minimize the risk of computer infections, there is no need to be paranoid to the point that you lose the pleasure and many of the benefits of computing. Allowing the virus threat to seriously inhibit networking, for example, can be more damaging than taking a calculated risk after adopting basic preventive measures.

Above all, remember that computer infections can be ultimately more under our control than many of the biological viruses that can infect our bodies. We do not yet have a quick technological fix, the silver bullet, or the magic pill for an instant cure, but we do have a comprehensive armory of defenses and remedies. An infection from a computer virus need never be fatal to a system where adequate precautions with its vital records have been taken and the recovery procedures detailed in this book have been implemented. You can nearly always resuscitate a computer and get its heart ticking smoothly again with a few key commands!

CHAPTER

3

The Twenty Questions Most Often Asked about Computer Viruses

"Is it true," a reporter asked me during the media panic over the Columbus Day virus, "that I can buy a device to put in the hole in the middle of my diskettes so that they cannot get infected by viruses? I've heard that these computing condoms work well."

This is by no means the most uninformed question ever asked about viruses by those lacking computing knowledge, although it does rank as one of the most entertaining. Indeed, there can be no stupid questions about what viruses are and how we should combat them. Computer viruses have become a phenomenon so far beyond our previous experience of mechanical and electronic processes that even the most basic questions must be addressed.

Computer technology has now passed outside the sphere of the experts to become a tool that almost anyone can use without special expertise. We live in a high-tech age, but the majority of us have little understanding of how our high-tech tools and toys operate. There are video cassette recorders in 80 percent of the homes in America, but surveys show that most of us do not know how to operate all of the controls on these machines. President Ronald Reagan, who controlled more technological power than any human being before him, admitted he found it difficult to switch on his own VCR—and impossible to turn it off!

Other computer users and those responsible for data processing activities have been reluctant to pose basic questions for fear of displaying embarrassing ignorance. This is an additional communications complication that managers must bear in mind when trying to educate computer users about viruses and the threat they pose to vital records and the functioning of business enterprises. Nowadays it can be damaging to career prospects for an employee to display ignorance about computing, as it has become a subject about which so many of us are now either expected or assumed to be knowledgeable. I remember being treated with near derision by management colleagues because I did not know how to use Lotus 1-2-3, which some consider essential equipment for scaling corporate ladders.

So we are tempted to pretend to understand more than we do about computers—and therein lies a serious danger to corporate systems, for concealed ignorance has the potential to do great harm. The virus epidemic was able to gather momentum and infect so many Fortune 500 companies largely because many computer and security experts have been painfully slow to understand what viruses are, why they are created, and what dangers they pose.

One of the biggest stumbling blocks in the late eighties to getting any kind of concerted action moving against the spread of viruses was trying to persuade the experts to admit their ignorance about the basic facts. Many have not displayed the open mind of the veteran software engineer with over two decades of programming experience who came up to me after I had given a short seminar on computer viruses in Long Beach. My audience consisted mostly of ordinary computer users, and so my presentation concentrated on basic, simple issues. Afterwards, the programmer told me that this was the first time he had really understood what viruses were all about and appreciated the dangers they posed. Let's hope we see more experts who will admit they do not know everything and that their very expertise may have blinkered their perceptions!

Now here are the answers to some basic questions most often asked about computer viruses. They are nontechnical in scope because you need little technical knowledge of computing to understand what viruses are, what they can do, and how to defend your system against most of them. In fact, computer viruses are not really a technical problem, but a human issue—one which will only be solved by the combined efforts of technical and human resources mixed with a liberal dose of common sense.

1 *What is a computer virus?*

A computer virus is a software program with the ability to repro-duce, or *clone*, itself. It may or may not damage data or other programs. A virus cannot do anything that was not written into its program. It is the intellectual creation of a human computer programmer, just like your word processing program, spreadsheet, or space invaders game. Several other types of harmful programs exist, such as worms and Trojan Horses, that are often called viruses in media reports. But a program is not a virus unless it has this ability to replicate. Often a virus will be hidden in a Trojan Horse—a damaging program disguised as an innocent one.

2 *Why would anyone want to create a computer virus?*

Writing a program that will assume a life of its own and spread, reproduce, and carry out the tasks that you instruct it to do is a fascinating intellectual challenge. For computer technology to continue its develop-ment, we need imaginative, creative people to experiment with and ex-plore the potential of the technology. Creating self-replicating programs is an important part of this development process, especially if we are to reap the full potential of computing to take on even more challenging tasks. Consequently, many viruses are created by responsible researchers or ex-perimenters, and these sometimes escape accidentally into the general computing environment. (See question 4 for information about innocuous viruses.)

Other viruses are created as pranks that misfire. Such a virus has the potential to do great harm if its program contains bugs that make it behave in a damaging way, especially if that virus spreads its infection indiscriminately.

Viruses have also provided a weapon for those members of society who wish to harm others for a variety of reasons. Some of these people are mischievous or destructive vandals, others have political points to make, and still others want to sabotage governments, organiza-tions, or companies that they feel have done them wrong.

Because the computing population has become so big, there now exists a significant number of vandals, sick minds, and people alienated from the mainstream who have the necessary skills to express their feelings by spreading viruses.

There is the copycat phenomenon to consider as well—for example, one case of someone putting poison into a proprietary medicine can lead to others imitating that action. Unlike drug tampering, however, you cannot stop the spread of copycat virus activity by putting tamper-proof seals on software packaging. Also, virus creation grows by going beyond simple copycat activity to actually inspiring someone to create a better virus. The Hypercard virus of 1988, the first to be written in the HyperTalk language, appeared to have been inspired by the MacMag Virus—both carried messages of peace and goodwill and did not reflect any deliberate intent to cause harm. But both have since been hacked (modified or improved) into different and more dangerous viruses.

Particularly intriguing is the possibility of virus creation being a new manifestation of the antagonism felt by some hackers against the way computers are being used by big business, government agencies, and other establishment symbols. Computing is a passion that dominates the lives of many enthusiasts. For some, that passion can develop into obsessional behavior, creating irrational motives to wreak revenge against those perceived to be abusing the "purity" of computing concepts.

Jealousy and a sense of inferiority can also play a role in shaping a hacker's attitudes. A maverick hacker who has difficulty relating to people and the real physical world feels that he must protect the computing environment, in which he functions comfortably, from being controlled by the very individuals and groups he resents. By disrupting systems and destroying data, he demonstrates that he is in control and has tangible power in territory that he regards as his personal space.

3 Why are viruses now spreading so rapidly? Do we have an epidemic running out of control?

As we have just seen, more people are creating new viruses and, at the same time, a compound growth continues in the number of viruses already in the computing environment that are replicating on their own or being spread deliberately. Anyone with a computer hooked up to another by telephone or connected to a network, or who exchanges disks with someone else or transports disks from one system to another, may either knowingly or innocently spread viruses.

Much of the spread is from infected systems that have not yet displayed symptoms. Many viruses work in the background while appearing to be doing something else. These viruses look for other files and disk drives to infect, even other addresses of people and systems they can visit next, hitching a free ride on your connections. They continue to replicate and find new victims invisibly, so the spread of infection is often far greater than it appears to be.

A computer virus that gets into a network can breed and spread more rapidly than the most prolific living entities. For example, the *Escherichia coli* bacterium that flourishes in our intestines can divide once every 15 minutes, but it is a sluggard compared to a computer virus—a computer virus can replicate itself several times in less than a second!

VIRUS FACT

If you suspect a new program might be infected but still decide to risk running it, and you do not have anti-viral software, try first to open it as read-only data files in a word processor. Look to see if there are unusual or rude messages among the programming instructions. Such messages are a feature of many viruses. But be warned! This action in itself may release the virus.

The rate of virus spread is limited by the opportunities for fresh infection; fortunately these are always restrained in some way or other. It is not a perfect world even for computer viruses, but their opportunities to replicate and do damage will only increase as more computer systems come into use, networking with each other and increasing in their compatibility for the exchange of programming code. One consequence of this increased compatibility between operating systems could be the spread of new versions of viruses from DOS-based systems to the Mac, Apple, Amiga, Atari, Unix and other computing environments. Even now these viruses can infect different systems by being converted into substrains that will flourish in other operating system environments.

A particularly disturbing possibility is the development of computer viruses that can mutate, just as some physical viruses and bacteria do. When these "super viruses" find their ability to replicate and survive inhibited, they adapt and change to fit the inhospitable environment. Already there are virus programs that can flourish within certain antiviral software designed to attack them. This is the equivalent of some types of insects becoming not just resistant to insecticides, but able to flourish on them.

4 *Why can an innocuous virus created for research or experiment be damaging?*

The first and primary task that a virus is programmed to execute is to clone itself. That is the very nature of this type of program, and it may take a very deliberate action by the creator to inhibit that cloning capability.

Even if the originator puts in controls to limit the rate of reproduction, these controls may fail. This happened when a German student sent friends an electronic Christmas card that infected IBM's international network. The IBM system virtually seized up when this virus kept cloning and sending itself to any address it could find. The Internet/Arpanet networks in the United States were disrupted by a similar overloading process caused by a program that had no deliberate malicious destructiveness written into it.

In a welcoming computing environment, such as a clean system or network, a virus can make a very large number of copies of itself very quickly. One virus suddenly becomes hundreds, thousands, maybe even millions. An innocuous virus can be destructive just by this very act of replication—expanding to the point where it clogs up a system with breeding activity, leaving no capacity for other tasks.

5 *Why is it so important—and difficult—to eliminate a virus completely from an infected system?*

If you leave just one clone in your system, once you have completed whatever virus disinfectant process you are using, the clone can reactivate and resume replicating, returning your system to an overwhelming level of infection in just a few seconds.

Remember that the viruses may not be visible. They may be hidden among other lines of coding, split up into bits and scattered here and there, but ready to come together when the opportunity arises. Some will conceal themselves within areas of the disk that they flag as "bad sectors," so that the system, an applications program, and even some virus detectors will not look there for either normal or virus coding. These fragments of virus coding are like black, oil-contaminated grains of sand scattered among the white grains on a beautiful, tranquil beach. The beach looks clean and normal, but nonetheless it has a concealed destructive element.

6 *What systems are most at risk from viruses?*

The DOS environment is the most common, and consequently this is where most infections occur. (The two dominant personal computer operating systems—PC-DOS from IBM and MS-DOS from Microsoft—are very similar, so we can apply the generic term *DOS* to any DOS-based IBM or compatible operating system, each of which are vulnerable to the same strains of viruses.) Not only is DOS the most common operating system, it is also the one in which most viruses are being created.

Other operating systems, such as OS/2, are growing increasingly vulnerable to viruses as they become more numerous, though not just because the installed base is expanding. There is a growing trend towards developing systems designed to appeal to network users, which creates more networks to provide places for viruses to spread. One advantage of OS/2 and other new systems is that they have some intrinsic barriers to virus infection, but these are not sufficient at this time to make OS/2—or any other system—immune.

Fewer people use Macs, Amigas, Commodores, and other proprietary systems, so these computing environments have fewer viruses. Also, these systems are less popular than DOS among virus creators. While Mac owners tend to think they do not have much of a virus problem, the Mac viruses can be more destructive than those in DOS systems because all Mac applications programs tend to run in similar ways, offering similar welcoming environments for a virus designed to replicate in them.

Ironically, the pre-DOS personal computer standard, CP/M, is comparatively free from viruses because few self-replicating programs existed when CP/M was popular, and the hackers have moved on to DOS and beyond. If you are really neurotic about viruses, you feel safer in the CP/M environment, where there is still a remarkably wide selection of great programs, and good used hardware is incredibly cheap.

7 Why don't viruses attack minis and mainframes as much as PCs?

Mainframes and minis are less vulnerable to viruses for several reasons, but they are very important in spreading viruses to personal computers. The bigger computers often cost millions of dollars each and tend to be custom designed to some degree so they can execute specific tasks most efficiently. Because they represent such a substantial investment, they are usually located in secure places with controlled access. These computers have security built into them, and they continue to be protected against all kinds of threats throughout their operational lives.

This does not make mainframes or minis immune to viruses, simply much less likely to get infected, especially since most viruses are created in DOS and therefore unable to attack mainframes directly. A virus's main targets are the thousands of PCs linked to the mainframes in one way or another, so all the virus needs to do to reach its objective is pass through the mainframe to get to the networked PCs. There are many human infections that use hosts in this way to get from one victim to another without actually harming the host or carrier that offers them temporary sanctuary and a free ride.

Think of the DOS virus's relationship with the mainframe as analogous to a terrorist gang's use of a railway terminus as a central location for distributing bombs. The gang leader takes a number of bombs to the terminus and leaves them in the luggage lockers. Other members of the gang come along, pick up their bombs, and catch different trains out of the terminus to the targeted locations. Later there are bomb explosions in several distant cities, but the terminus is not affected, nor is it even threatened at any time. You can consider the mainframe computer to be the equivalent of the railway terminus, the PCs to be the distant targets, and the viruses to play both the traveling terrorists who carry the bombs to the targets as well as the bombs themselves—with the ability to destroy data instead of buildings.

Despite the lack of virus infection on minis and mainframes, these large computers remain a challenge to which virus creators are increasingly responding. They are writing more sophisticated, intelligent viruses that can adapt to the different mainframe operating systems and structures and overcome the security procedures. With the spread of languages used on minis and mainframes, these computers will become more accessible to the virus creators and a more tempting medium in which to write viruses.

Viruses can also exploit the customized nature of the biggest computer systems. Someone wishing to sabotage a government or big corporate system can secretly disseminate a virus that will replicate very efficiently in DOS systems, but remain hidden and not do any damage until it passes from the DOS environment to the specific mini or mainframe system at which it is targeted.

This strategy could be very effective for anyone wanting to cause maximum damage to a computer-dependent society, and is willing to wait. With this method, the virus replicates to the point where its sheer spread throughout the computing universe steadily increases the odds that at some time, somehow, it will find its way into the targeted system. This is a kind of computer germ warfare in which many would be harmed. The first example of the resources able to commit this kind of electronic sabotage against governments and the business and academic communities may have been the hostile AIDS program that first appeared in December 1989. (See Chapter 8.)

8   *Are viruses difficult to create?*

It's getting easier all the time! Virus creation programs exist that help a person with limited computer expertise create viruses by providing menu options for large sections of the program coding. This eliminates the need to write much of the actual virus code, opening the door to the fast, easy, and comparatively unskillful creation of viruses—a most disturbing development.

Some viruses are fairly easy to program from scratch, while others require extensive software engineering expertise. As computer literacy has increased, hundreds of thousands of people now have sufficient knowledge to write viruses. It is inevitable that among this increase in computer literates are those with malicious motives.

9   *What can viruses do?*

From the merely amusing to the absolutely disastrous, there is practically no limit to what a virus can do to affect computing activity. Some of the more discreet activities can have the worst consequences because the user may not be aware for a long time that anything is going wrong. In the worst cases, the ability of viruses to corrupt medical records, air traffic control systems, and other safety-critical computing operations means that these hostile programs could actually kill.

Viruses can alter just a small bit of data here and there, such as adding a zero to multiply certain figures by ten or moving a decimal point a place or two, either in a carefully calculated or a random manner. In text files, a virus may change one name for another, or whenever a particular name crops up, add an obscenity to it. There actually is a virus targeted at word processing and electronic editing systems that adds obscenities to the names of specific right-wing political leaders, including President Ronald Reagan, Prime Minister Margaret Thatcher, and President Pieter Botha.

It is not difficult to create a virus that would alter particular words or phrases to achieve changes in meaning that the computer user would not spot until too late. It could, for example, be most damaging to have obscenities discreetly inserted or certain phrases changed or added to your document at the stage of data processing when you perform a mail merge or process a batch of form letters. The lack of human monitoring at this stage could enable the virus activity to go undetected—until the letters reach their recipients, of course!

Mass mailings are now such a routine operation that an undetected virus might, for example, be able to add text to every 100th form letter without it being noticed. A disgruntled employee or a saboteur working for a competitor might insert a virus that would add a postscript that says, "Of course, everything in the above is lies," or append to a Republican appeal for funds a plug for Democratic political objectives. The possibilities for exploiting the ability of viruses to discreetly modify text and numbers is virtually limitless and could be very damaging.

Many viruses slow computing operations down because of the sheer load that their reproductive activity imposes, particularly if there are bugs in the virus. But they can also be made to do this deliberately in various ways, either to annoy or to make the system virtually unusable. This slowing down ability could take the form of product sabotage. For example, you could make your rival's spreadsheet so slow to implement cell changes that it frustrates its users, creating a marketing opportunity for your spreadsheet program.

Viruses also can be used to steal data, and stolen data can be used to steal other, more tangible property—you have to steal the key to the cookie cupboard before you can steal the cookies. For example, suppose a hacker breaks into a corporate system, and creates a hidden or disguised account or file, creating an opportunity to introduce a virus. The virus can roam through the system, cloning itself to increase its capacity to search through the records of different departments, or of any other systems connected to the network. These clones can gather confidential data on employees, the results of research and development activities, new product marketing plans, secret formulas, details of merger or acquisition strategies, or any other valuable data—without anyone's knowledge except the invader's. This information is then copied automatically to the hidden file, where the invader can collect and analyze it at will.

The analogy here is to a burglar breaking into a corporate headquarters and then cloning into hundreds of other burglars who start ransacking the filing cabinets and confidential records throughout the building, secretly making copies of anything interesting and putting the original documents back exactly where they were so that when the staff come in the next day they do not suspect that anything untoward has happened. All those copies are taken to the leader of the gang, who then transmits them though a telephone link out of the building to a designated location anywhere in the world.

A very simple routine to program a virus to do is to execute a normal DOS routine at the most inopportune time so that it causes the most harm. For example, when you save a file, the virus might change the command to FORMAT, destroying all the data on the disk to which you intended to save your work.

As well as changing commands, viruses may also redefine the very keys with which you try to issue those commands. DOS and some applications programs have the facility to make, say, the "A" key act as the "Z" key. Many applications programs now enable you to create single-key macros—you hit just one key once and it triggers off a whole keyboard sequence. A virus can be programmed to do any of those things, scrambling your keystroke definition table or creating destructive macros.

Imagine the chaos and losses in a large organization with networked computers if there was a virus running wild that converts all the usual QWERTY keyboards to the Dvorak layout. The victims would be confused and unable to function. Everything would grind to a halt. It's bad enough when only one key does not work effectively, as happens when cigarette ash falls into the keyboard and causes malfunctions. Imagine what would happen if all the keys on all the keyboards throughout a network were scrambled.

Another tricky tactic adopted by some viruses is to scramble the File Allocation Table (FAT). The FAT plays the role of your system's index, telling it where the different files are located. A virus can take all this information and mix it up, rather like dumping a tray of library index cards onto the floor, scrambling them into a random sequence so it becomes almost impossible to find a book's title, and so locate it on the shelves. Some viruses go even further and scramble the file names also. This is the equivalent of changing the covers on all the books in the library to make locating any particular one even worse than seeking a needle hidden in a haystack.

A virus is also an effective communications tool when programmed to disseminate messages to any system it manages to infect. We have only just started to see viruses used for propaganda of various kinds, from racist slogans to support for the legalization of marijuana, as in the New Zealand virus's screen display:

Legalize marijuana. Your computer is now stoned.

10 Can a virus damage hardware?

The ability of viruses to damage hardware or pose any kind of physical risk to operators periodically attracts popular media attention and has been grossly exaggerated. In theory, a virus could cause your hard disk to continually spin until it either failed or perhaps overheated, caught fire, and burned the house down. But that is a most unlikely scenario.

Some types of monitors may be damaged by a virus repeatedly sending a bright signal to one location on the screen. There is a particular product model of a well-known brand of hard disk that is prone to failure because of a weak electronic component. It is conceivable that a virus could be written to generate intensive read-write activity that would hasten the failure of that hardware.

In reality, it is virtually impossible for software to damage hardware without the user being aware that something is wrong long before physical damage can occur. The operating life of a hard disk might be reduced a few hundred hours by viral activity, but only if the computer with the hard disk was left unattended for an extended period and no one observed any strange behavior on it.

Viruses are only a form of software, so they will primarily damage other software or data. But that's bad enough, since the software and the data that it creates are far more valuable to most computer users than the actual physical machinery.

Of course, physical damage could result from virus contamination of computers that control machinery, such as a robot welder or spray painter in an automobile or appliance manufacturing plant. Such equipment incorporates so many fail-safe procedures that discrepancies in the control data are usually detected. However, corruption of the control data might not be so readily visible with certain sensitive activities, such as the measurement of components going into chemical products, manufactured foods, and pharmaceuticals.

11   *Is it now dangerous to use electronic mail?*

The ability of viruses to damage electronic mail has also been exaggerated. Because this communications traffic is predominantly data and not programming, it provides few and difficult opportunities for viruses to either hide or spread infection.

Electronic mail systems that only transmit data back and forth in the form of ASCII text are now comparatively safe from potentially damaging phenomena. There is a significant risk of infection only on systems that permit executable files to be transferred.

Despite the fact that viruses cannot actually infect data, only destroy or modify it, they can travel with data; viruses can be constructed to activate and transmit themselves when an electronic line is opened and software is used to carry out the data transfer. While viruses attach themselves to and hide in programs, being programs in their own right, they include instructions to disseminate themselves with certain types of data transfers that may contain programming code.

12   *What is the most common type of DOS virus?*

A large proportion of DOS viruses are created as boot sector infectors that search out .COM or .EXE files. These files are present in virtually every DOS system, and so make readily available and comparatively easy targets. Particularly attractive are the hidden system files—DOS files that are not listed in the directory, and so are easier to infect without revealing that an infection has taken place. (See Chapters 2 and 6.)

Many DOS viruses hide in the clock device, as this part of the system usually runs as soon as the system is switched on. This way the virus may be activated before any antiviral program begins to check the system. Many viruses are time activated—they contain the equivalent of built-in time fuses and will scan the internal clock to find out if the current time and date coincide with its programmed instructions.

13 *What are Terminate and Stay Resident viruses and why are they so troublesome?*

A Terminate and Stay Resident program (TSR) remains in memory after it has carried out a task, ready to activate again if you need it. Shell or clock programs are oftentimes TSR programs, and so are some viruses. Once a TSR virus gets into a system and has carried out its initial infections, it hides in RAM and waits for new opportunities to infect (for instance, when you load a disk or hook up to another system over a network). Even without being activated, a TSR virus can cause malfunctions simply by occupying space in RAM, which may prevent some applications programs from running. A TSR virus may also conflict with programs in some other way, not just by taking up the RAM space that they need.

This viral activity creates mysterious symptoms that may be blamed on software bugs or hardware malfunctions, giving the virus more opportunity to spread before it is detected.

14 *Can I protect my system from time-delay viruses by setting my computer's clock calendar far forward into the future? Or can I turn the clock back so that it will not activate the virus?*

The clock device is a favorite virus hiding place. This part of the system usually runs as soon as the system is switched on, so the virus may be activated before an antiviral program begins to check for virus activity. Viruses that scan the CMOS storage to find out if the current time and date match the time and date they have been programmed to activate on are becoming more common. So also is the modification of time-delay viruses, so that a virus first identified to activate on, say, the Fourth of July may quickly be hacked into a version that will trigger on July 1, and so catch more victims.

Such tricks as changing your clock and calendar settings may work in some situations, but it is not a reliable defense. A time-delay virus is usually set to activate at any point after a certain date or time, so you may set it off immediately by moving your clock and calendar settings forward.

15 *How can viruses prevent you from accessing your data, even if the data is not destroyed?*

There are two ways in which DOS organizes your files, and both are vulnerable to virus attack. The first is the logical ordering that you can control by directories, subdirectories, and paths that make particular programs available in a particular order. Viruses find a happy hunting ground in directories and subdirectories where they can make files inaccessible by making it *appear* that they have been destroyed without actually damaging them. This type of damage requires less programming than destroying data records, and so makes the virus more compact and consequently less likely to be seen. It is also a way of disguising virus activity—keeping the user in blissful ignorance of infection. The message "File not found" may not mean that the data in the field is lost or damaged, but that a virus has altered the directory to make it difficult, if not impossible, to find where that file is located.

The second file organizing system is the DOS File Allocation Table (FAT), the peculiar and often inefficient way in which DOS stores files in bits and pieces anywhere there is space on the disk to accommodate them. A given file may be broken up into bits all over the place; only the FAT knows where the pieces are and can ensure that, when you want that file, all the bits are found and brought together in the right order. (You can tell how this storage system works by the way the hard disk spins and the head scans back and forth to collect all the bits in a long file.) This process takes longer as the hard disk fills up, because there is more information for the FAT to search through to find the elements of the file you seek. Disk utilities exist that will constructively organize these bits physically closer together to make them easier to collect. A virus that attacks the FAT will also reorganize things, but in a destructive way so that you cannot find them. (You can yourself cause the same disastrous effect if you incorrectly use a utility that can modify the FAT.)

16 *How does a checksum warn you of virus infections?*

The checksum, or snapshot, is rather like a fingerprint or identity number for a program or file. It is a numerical record of the size of a program or file in its uninfected state, and you use this as a baseline figure that you can check from time to time. If the number changes, it may indicate that a virus infection has occurred. Some antiviral and utility programs will do this for you automatically. However, some viruses will automatically override the checksum process to conceal their presence.

17 *Why do bulletin boards spread viruses so readily?*

Bulletin boards, like parties, are great places to meet new friends, acquire information, and pick up nasty infections if you are not careful.

Already there are over 30,000 bulletin boards in the United States, and we can expect this number to grow dramatically as more individuals and organizations realize how useful it is to set up these electronic meeting places. Bulletin boards used to be almost the sole preserve of computing enthusiasts. Now even a small company or individual can set up a board with minimum cost and trouble. For as little as $50 in software (or nothing if you use one of the excellent public domain or shareware programs available) plus a PC clone with a hard disk and a telephone line, you can have a bulletin board up and running in no time at very little cost.

The business community is becoming increasingly dependent on bulletin boards as a way to communicate with sales or other staff away from base. Bulletin boards are an essential element of the important trend towards telecommuting. The "electronic cottage" and other such manifestations of the changing work environment make it possible for employees as well as independent contractors to work more from home or other locations distant from a central facility.

Bulletin boards are becoming very important to nearly all of us in so many ways. They are already a great bargain, and as costs drop, their numbers and use will increase. Indeed, bulletin boards will become such a vital means of communication that if viruses did nothing else but threaten them, we would have a very serious problem.

Because their very purpose is to act as a medium for the exchange of data (and often programs), bulletin boards are very vulnerable to virus infection. But do not let the virus epidemic scare you away from the wonderful world of the bulletin boards, just as many of us have been frightened away from many of our urban parks and downtown areas after dark. In the same way you would be careful in any urban area, be careful when using unfamiliar bulletin board services.

18 *Why is there not a universal virus vaccine to prevent infection, or the equivalent of a broad spectrum antibiotic to catch and treat the different strains of viruses?*

The answer is obvious if you remember that viruses are not a new and different aspect of computing activities, but simply programs. Consequently, they behave in most respects like normal, healthy programs. So any "medicine" designed to wipe out the viruses could also damage normal computing activities, rather like an herbicide that kills both the weeds and the plants. Also, to destroy many of the viruses around, this "medicine" would have to be so potent that it could damage your computing system, just as some cancer and AIDS treatments are difficult to use effectively because they destroy healthy as well as infectious cells.

Fortunately, there are antiviral programs that strike a practical compromise between these conflicting requirements, but they must be updated all the time. An out-of-date antiviral program is about as useful as last season's influenza shot. The thrust and parry between those creating and those trying to defeat viruses is an ongoing fight in which the defensive tactics must be continually modified to meet attacks coming from new directions.

So you need to have either a new antiviral program or one that you can update regularly. ViruScan, which is included on the disk that accompanies this book, is an example of a utility that regularly takes the temperature of your system and warns you if it is getting sick and needs treatment.

19 *Why do even humorous or benign viruses get out of control and do things that the originator did not intend?*

Viruses are software programs, so chances are that they will contain *bugs*, or programming errors, just like any other software. It is almost impossible for even the biggest software publishers with virtually unlimited testing resources to produce programs that are completely bug free. Some publishers think they are doing well if the first versions of a new program that they release have an error rate better than 3 percent. The virus programmer, almost invariably operating alone without the major publisher's facilities for checking a new program, is likely to have a higher error rate varying by the size and complexity of the program.

Cause and effect are not always clearly related, and this complicates the situation even further. A mistake in one part of the program might cause an error to arise in a competely different place. Sometimes the effect in one particular system with its particular hardware configuration or software utilities can be completely different from what will occur in another system.

Any programming mistakes can form bugs that cause the program to do things that are not intended. A computer requires perfectly precise instructions, in contrast to human comprehension, which enables us to extract the essential meaning from documentation that may be littered with spelling, grammar, and punctuation mistakes.

The bugs in your software—even if it is a very well-known brand—may create symptoms very similar to those of a virus infection. Similarly, if you get a virus attack in your system, the bugs in its program may create symptoms that have not previously been identified in other experiences with the same virus.

Software bugs in both legitimate programs and viruses can cause data loss in virtually identical ways—from losing a few bytes of information to the destruction of all the data on a disk. Sometimes the data will only be corrupted, which can be more damaging than its destruction if you do not know what is happening. On other occasions, a bug will make data appear to be destroyed when in fact it is still there, and your reactions may then cause it to be destroyed.

Some virus bugs occur in the delivery or replication instruction sections of the program. These can make a virus hit computers that it did not originally target, as happened with the Scores virus. This Mac virus was originally written to infect only those systems running databases processing information relating to the Electronic Data Systems corporation. But a bug in the Scores virus caused it to run amok throughout the Mac computing environment, reaching systems in NASA, Congress—even Apple's own computers in the company's Washington offices.

A bug in the Israeli or Jerusalem virus caused it to replicate out of control, continually reinfecting files it had already infected once. That bug had beneficial effects because it gave a warning of virus activity before the data destruction section of the coding had an opportunity to activate fully.

A bug in the worm program that Robert Morris, Jr. released into the Internet network effectively removed the brakes that Morris had put there to stop his program from doing extensive damage. Like a runaway truck, it ploughed its way through the Defense Communications Agency's networks, disabling 6,000 systems and creating direct and indirect damage that has been estimated by the Computer Virus Industry Association at over $100 million.

Computing enthusiasts enjoy finding the bugs in virus programs and putting them right. So viruses get tweaked and fine-tuned as they spread around the computing community, evolving to become more effective just as a new commercial software product improves by having its bugs worked out.

However, removing a bug from a virus program—or deliberately altering that program—may have a snowball effect that can disrupt the whole concept and internal logic of the program. Any tampering with a virus has potential dangers that are not readily apparent. That is why the creator of the virus simulation programs on the disk that accompanies this book, Joe Hirst, has added coding to them so that they cannot be altered.

20

As viruses may spread to backup copies, is there any completely secure way in which to preserve data that is priceless to me?

Yes, but until something better is created, it means going back to conventional printing on paper. If you have data that you *must* preserve, then print it out in a form that can be scanned easily. Don't use fancy fonts or formatting. Create a hard copy in the typeface and layout that can be most accurately read by one of the many optical scanning devices now available.

You don't even need to own a scanner. Make your archival hard copies in the appropriate format and store them securely as described in Chapter 10. Then, if all your computerized data is lost because of a virus infection or any other reason, you can bring out your hard copies and either have them scanned by someone else or buy yourself a scanner at that point. The equipment can cost as little as $200. That can seem a remarkable value as you see your hard copy brought back into electronic form and data otherwise permanently lost is restored, healthy and ready to be processed again.

CHAPTER

4

Simulating a Virus Attack

Reading about a virus attack and experiencing one are two very different things. As you now know, computer virus infections and hardware or software failures can display very similar symptoms, so unless you've actually seen a virus in action, it may be difficult to know exactly what type of problem you are experiencing.

In this chapter you are introduced to the Virus Simulation Suite programs found on the disk accompanying this book. Joe Hirst, director of the British Computer Virus Research Centre and editor of the newsletter *The Virus Vigil*, has created these programs to enable you to experience the symptoms of a virus attack without putting your system at risk. Once you see how a virus actually behaves, you will be better prepared to respond if you are unfortunate enough to be a victim of the real thing.

These programs can also be very useful training aids, and Hirst encourages people to copy and disseminate these programs to educate other users so long as the programs are not altered in any way.

This chapter provides an overview of the Virus Simulation Suite, a description of each of the programs, and step-by-step instructions for running them on a PC system. No such simulations of Mac or Amiga viruses are available.

If you have any questions about the virus simulations, or want to know more about the British Computer Virus Research Centre and its *Virus Vigil* newsletter, you can contact Joe Hirst at 12 Guildford Street, Brighton, East Sussex BN1 3LS ENGLAND, U.K. The telephone number from North America is 011-44 273 26105.

≈ What Is the Virus Simulation Suite?

These programs simulate the visual effects of several common computer viruses. You can run the simulation programs with confidence because they only mimic the action of viruses without actually doing any damage.

Some of the demonstrations are "single-shot," giving a one-time display. Others continue simulating the on-screen symptoms of a virus infection. Some take a long time to activate, waiting for you to carry out the action that the real virus is programmed to respond to. All these virus simulation programs can be removed by a warm boot of your system or by pressing the Alt and minus keys simultaneously.

≈ The Virus Simulation Suite Programs

Here are descriptions of each of the programs in the Virus Simulation Suite. Six viruses are simulated, with three of these showing two types of displays.

CASC-SIM.COM—Cascade Virus

In this simulation of the Cascade virus, characters fall down the screen until they encounter another character or a change in the background or foreground colors.

The area of the screen affected is initially one column. This builds up with successive displays until the full screen is affected. The delay before the first display is random, with a maximum of five minutes. The following delays between displays are also random, with a maximum of one minute.

CSC-SIMX.COM [n]—Cascade Virus

This display-only simulation of the Cascade virus has a controlled delay. Characters fall down the screen until they encounter another character or a change in the background or foreground colors. The full screen area is affected. The delay before the first display and between displays is one minute; enter a parameter (n) to change the delay.

DENZ-SIM.COM—Denzuk Virus

This single-shot display is not a TSR program, nor does it accept any parameters. It duplicates the visual display produced by the Denzuk virus when Ctrl-Alt-Del is intercepted.

FUMN-SIM.COM—Fu Manchu Virus

The virus intercepts the keyboard I/O interrupt (the method by which the keyboard actions are transmitted to the computer for processing). When the virus recognizes certain words, it adds comments to them.

The trigger words include "Thatcher," "Botha," "Reagan," "Waldheim," and "Fu Manchu." In each case the trigger is the word (or words) followed by a space. The other trigger words are two explicit four-letter words (not followed by a space). Be warned that this simulation, like the virus, uses explicit language. (See "FUM-SIMX.COM" if you wish to run a censored version of this simulation.)

Ctrl-Alt-Del is also intercepted and produces a message before the machine reboots.

There is no reset with this program.

FUM-SIMD.COM—Fu Manchu Virus

This single-shot display is not a TSR program, nor does it accept any numeric delay parameters. It simply displays the message produced by the virus when Ctrl-Alt-Del is intercepted.

FUM-SIMX.COM—Fu Manchu Virus

This program is exactly as described for the FUMN-SIM.COM simulation, except that the two obscene words have been censored, both on input and output. This version is intended for public demonstrations where the "full-blooded" version would be inappropriate.

ITAL-SIM.COM—Italian Virus

This program simulates the action of the Italian virus, which causes a single character to become a "bouncing ball" on the screen. The action is similar to Ping Pong and other bouncing ball programs that have been widely disseminated among computers and different operating systems.

The display will only activate under the same conditions that trigger the real virus. If you perform a disk access during a "window" lasting one second in every half hour, the display will appear. "Reset" (Alt-+) will switch off the display again until the next such activation.

ITL-SIMX.COM [n]—Italian Virus

This display-only program runs a screen display of the Italian virus, which is a single character "bouncing ball."

If called with a parameter (n), there will be a delay before the display is activated equal to the parameter in minutes. "Reset" (Alt-+) will switch off the display until this same delay has elapsed again. If called without a parameter, the display will appear immediately. "Reset" will switch the display on and off.

JERU-SIM.COM [n]—Jerusalem Virus

This program simulates the Jerusalem virus. After the initial delay, a portion of the screen scrolls up two lines, creating a small, black gap in the display. At the same time, a time-wasting loop is activated, and the processor appears to be slowed down. "Reset" (Alt-+) will switch off the slow-down effect, and re-institute the delay.

If called with a parameter (*n*), there is a delay before the display is activated equal to the parameter in minutes. If called without a parameter, the delay is one minute. "Reset" will switch off the display until this same delay has elapsed again.

OROPAX.COM—Oropax Musical Virus

Sound effects were either absent from viruses, or very primitive, until the Oropax, an application program infector, began spreading in Europe and the United States in 1990. This simulation has built-in delays of between five and seven minutes. After loading, stand by for your computer to play *Stars and Stripes*, *Blue Danube*, or a familiar Mozart theme.

≈ Using the Virus Simulation Suite

The Virus Simulation Suite is easy to run. You may first need to transfer files from the enclosed 5¼" disk to a 3½" disk. Then, simply follow the instructions in this section to start the program.

Copying the Simulation Files to a 3 ½" Disk

If you want to run the simulations on a laptop or a system that uses only 3½" disks, you will need to transfer the files containing the simulations to a 3½" disk with file transfer software, a modem link, and so on. You can make a duplicate of the entire disk or copy each of the simulation files separately. Consult your DOS, hardware system, or file-transfer software manual if you are uncertain how to do this.

A way to move the programs from the original disk to a 3½" disk if you do not have transfer facilities is to send them by modem from a system that will run the original disk to one that will run 3½" disks.

Running the Simulation Programs

To run the simulation programs, place the disk in drive A and type in the file name of the virus you wish to simulate. Most of the simulations operate after about a minute, while others have a programmable time delay to make them more realistic. With the time-delayed simulations, you load one of the simulations and then carry on with some other computing task. The virus simulation will take place without warning sometime in the next 30 minutes. You can remove it immediately by pressing Alt--, although it is recommended that you do not do any important work with the simulation and TSR utilities in RAM in case there are any unpredictable reactions.

Many of these are Terminate and Stay Resident programs (TSR programs)—they load into RAM. They can be removed from memory by pressing Alt--. (On some laptops, you bring the – or + keys into action by using them in conjunction with the Num Lock key.)

You can both switch off and change the delay in some of the simulations by pressing Alt-+. The one-shot displays, such as the ITL-SIMX simulation of the Italian virus, do not have a time delay; Alt-+ switches these displays on and off.

Any program, particularly those that remain temporarily resident in RAM, may conflict with other programs being run at the same time or create unpredictable symptoms. There may also be unpredictable behavior on certain hardware. This can also occur with the virus simulations. For example, when I ran the Cascade simulation on an old IBM PC with a monochrome monitor, the keyboard locked up temporarily.

Do not be alarmed if you experience any surprises. These simulations are not viruses, and you can delete the program by following the instructions—usually just by pressing the Alt and minus keys at the same time. And you can always remove the simulation by a warm re-boot of your system.

CHAPTER

5

If Things Go Wrong, Don't Always Blame a Virus

During the eighties, computers increased rapidly in both value and reliability. As prices tumbled, so did the failure rate as both electronic circuits and the small proportion of mechanical components in personal computers were refined.

In the nineties, the pace of improvement will slow down considerably. The computing power you get for your buck should continue to increase steadily, though not quite at the rate we experienced in the eighties due to the economies of scale already being factored into selling prices. Reliability is now so good that there is not a lot of room for improvement in this area. However, system downtime will start to rise again as virus activity mitigates against the progress made in hardware design and manufacture.

We can expect more programs to crash, data to be lost, and hardware to malfunction as viruses spread and do their dirty work in more systems. But just because the hardware has become better and the viruses have become worse, don't bring yourself unnecessary anguish and stress by invariably assuming that your system has been infected whenever something goes wrong. If you take reasonable precautions to keep viruses out of your system, the chances of the problem being caused by a software bug or a hardware malfunction should be greater than from a virus.

In fact, if you look around your work space, you may well see hazards that you have introduced to your working environment that pose more of a risk than a virus infection. Just as viruses are a human problem, so are some of the other causes of computer failure.

≈ Take a Close Look at Your Bad Computing Habits

If there was an Environmental Protection Agency for computers, it might produce a check list for operators that includes the following questions about your workspace:

- Is that disk you were just using propped up against the telephone or resting on top of the monitor?
- Do you keep your paper clips nearby in one of those ingenious little boxes with a round magnet in the top?
- Have you dusted your workspace recently?
- Where is your coffee cup?
- Are you smoking or eating popcorn, nuts, or potato chips near your computer?
- Is sunlight streaming through a nearby window?
- Are your disks lying down on top of each other?
- Is the refrigerator, electric heater, washing machine, or air conditioner on the same electrical circuit as your system?
- Are your cables neatly coiled together?
- Have you a comfortable carpet on the floor?

If you can give an affirmative answer to any of these questions, you may be exposing your data to more risk than having a raunchy night out on the most promiscuous bulletin boards you can find. All of the questions point to unsafe computing practices that may cause symptoms very difficult to distinguish at first from various types of virus attacks.

Let's look at these common computer workspace hazards more closely.

Is that disk you were just using propped up against the telephone or resting on top of the monitor? Do you keep your paper clips nearby in one of those ingenious little boxes with a round magnet in the top?

Since programs and data are stored by means of controlled magnetism, they can be destroyed by maverick magnetic fields, of which there are many in the typical office or home.

There are literally millions of tiny magnets on a floppy disk, and even a weak magnetic field can disrupt the precise alignment necessary for these microscopic magnets to preserve data accurately. For example, the electromagnet in a phone generates quite strong magnetic fields when activated by an incoming call. Important data stored on a disk can be corrupted or destroyed in an instant if the disk is close to the phone when someone calls.

Magnetized paper clip holders are another frequent cause of data loss—they just don't belong anywhere on a desk with a computer system. If you have one of those copy holders with a magnetic clip to keep papers in place, throw it out—it is definitely hazardous to the health of your data. It is amazing that these are sold in reputable computer stores, although this is not the most surprising display of ignorance concerning the disastrous interaction of magnets and disks. A software publisher who should have known better sent out a demonstration disk and in the same package included as a promotional giveaway a magnetic note holder. This may have been the first recorded instance of self-destructing junk mail!

Tape recorders—especially the small pocket memos many of us use these days and which you often need to have at your desk—can easily become concealed under a pile of papers. The magnetic fields generated by a tape recorder's speaker or microphone can be powerful enough to cause substantial damage to any disks in close proximity. If a disk is adversely affected, the garbled programming or corrupted data might not be noticed for a long time, and so no clear link is established between the cause and effect. In this kind of situation, a virus can easily be suspected, and a lot of time could be wasted trying to track down an infection that isn't there.

Other sources of magnetic interlopers in your workspace include the monitor (especially if it is a color monitor), the printer, audio speakers and speaker phones, adding machines, electric typewriters, fans, and desk lamps (especially the fluorescent type with ballasts).

 ### *Have you dusted your workspace recently?*

If you have, you may well have aggravated the risks of your system malfunctioning from mechanical causes. Dust is the physical Public Enemy No. 1 as far as data is concerned, and absolute death to diskettes if it gets out of control.

Indiscriminate use of a feather duster, broom, or vacuum cleaner around a computer work station can spread dust particles, hairs, and the ash from cigarettes onto the surfaces of disks and read-write heads, causing physical damage or error readings. The problem is aggravated further as particles of oxide are dislodged from the disk surface, creating more pollution.

How well a disk resists physical attacks from dust, other environmental pollutants, and its own "dandruff" depends on the quality of its construction and how much it is both used and abused. Poorer quality disks tend to have thinner oxide coatings that are more easily dislodged (the rate of surface erosion usually being in inverse proportion to the cost of the disk), and there is usually a low-quality fiber lining in the jacket containing the disk. This lining is supposed to catch the bits of oxide generated inside, as well as any dust that gets past the outer defenses of jacket or case. In adverse conditions, especially with inferior disks, the liner becomes loaded with particles and dust to the point that it no longer functions properly, just as the air filter on an auto engine can clog up. Then, instead of the liner cleaning the disk, there is an abrasive action as the disk rotates and the destructive garbage spreads to the heads and to other disks. The read and write problems characteristic of some virus attacks may well arise from dust and dirt contamination in the disk drives. A section of the oxide surface can deteriorate to the point where data cannot be stored or recovered, resulting in a "drop out" effect (sections of the disk are temporarily unaccessible). This "drop out" effect is virtually identical to a virus symptom.

If you use one of those disk notchers that gives you access to the flip side of a single-sided diskette, you make the risk of physical damage much greater. The notcher works by cutting a small piece from the edge of the disk cover so that the disk is not write protected. The tool may seem to make a clean cut, but tiny bits of disk may scatter and cling to the disk surface. Using the other side of the disk requires that it be put into the drive bottom-side up. This reverses its direction of rotation and applies pressure to the magnetic surface and the liner, further increasing the likelihood that dust and other garbage will come off the liner onto the surface of the disk. Bleed-through corruption of data may occur also, with the magnetic forces created by the storage of data on one side of the disk bleeding through to affect the data on the reverse side.

Fingerprints are another major cause of malfunctioning disks. The oxide-coated surface should never be touched directly, and disks should always be handled by their outer jackets. Sometimes disk surfaces are accidentally touched, but most problems arise from careless handling or unconscious habit. Flicking the little metal shutter on microdisks backwards and forwards is a high-tech habit that for some has replaced paper clip bending.

Here is a more constructive habit: put the diskettes back into their paper sleeves whenever they are out of the drive and stack them vertically in a nonmetallic case that will protect them from dust and other environmental threats. Vertical stacking is quite important because it reduces the likelihood of physical damage or dust penetration. Disks carelessly left lying around are more likely to get bent and have things put on top of them, possibly resulting in the liner and disk binding against each other. Any of these causes of physical damage can result in symptoms similar to the electronic damage from some viral infections.

Magnetic storage media are also vulnerable, and when the computer encounters a bad sector on a disk, it cannot tell you whether the damage was caused by a virus wreaking havoc on your system or the operator using a ballpoint instead of a felt-tip pen to write on a label already mounted on a disk. Labels and disks do not come separately just to save on manufacturing costs!

Dust buildup inside the computer or printer can also contribute to overheating problems, static electricity, short circuits, chip failures, and other operational woes which may be confused with the symptoms of viral infection, especially if the problems are intermittent. Monitors and other highly charged electrical components literally act as magnets for dust and other particles, so a periodic internal cleanup of your computer and peripherals is well worthwhile.

Keeping the area around the computer clean makes sense. When your workspace does get dirty, clean up with a slightly damp cloth or sponge rather than vigorously dusting. Dust will be kept under control more effectively if you apply an antistatic spray carefully, such as a 20 percent solution of fabric softener, to the outside cases of your hardware. In dusty working conditions, plastic or fabric covers for the hardware are essential. My whole system was once saved from serious damage by its flimsy plastic dust covers. I was away for the weekend when the roof of my house developed a leak during a heavy storm and water dripped through the ceiling over my desk. Water wrecked the hard copies on my desk, but my computer and the data stored there remained dry under the inexpensive little tents.

Suspect a buildup of grime in disk drives (especially in older systems) that fail to read or write to disk. This may be far easier to fix and prevent from recurring than trying to tackle a nonexistent viral infection.

Manual cleaning of the read-write heads is not as difficult as it seems, but don't be tempted to dip a Q-tip into a glass of gin or vodka and poke it through the disk slot in the hope of shifting the dirt that is causing your problem. Don't laugh at the thought of such foolishness—that's just what I had to do years ago with my old CP/M system at a location site in Africa with no expertise or proper materials available. It worked as a quick fix, but it would have been better to use a proper kit with lint-free swabs and denatured alcohol or special solvent. If you do decide to clean the read-write heads, be aware that some disassembly of the computer and the drives is necessary for manual cleaning and should not be attempted without either technical know-how or a good manual that gives detailed, step-by-step instructions.

The easiest way to clean the inside of your disk drive (though not quite as thorough as using a manual cleaning kit) is to run a head-cleaning diskette in your system. Pick a reliable brand that is nonabrasive. Follow the instructions explicitly, being particularly careful about the application of solvent and the time that the cleaning disk is run. Using too little or too much solvent and leaving the disk in for as little as 15 to 20 seconds too long can do more harm than not cleaning at all.

The experts differ on the advisability of using disk cleaners as preventive medicine. They are so easy to use that it is no problem to run them weekly, monthly, or two or three times a year depending on the manufacturer's recommendations and the intensity of computer usage. I myself follow the school that says leave the disks alone in ordinary circumstances and wait until there are read-write errors before cleaning the heads.

One last word about disk drives: Do not be too concerned about strange noises. Some viruses can cause frenzied disk activity, and this is a cause for concern, especially if the time that it takes for the disk to perform a task is excessive. But often a disk will whir and growl in an alarming way without anything at all being wrong. You may notice that some brands of floppies are noisier than others, which may not be a bad thing. The noise may indicate that the liner is efficiently keeping the oxide surface clean, while another disk is quieter simply because it has a less efficient liner.

Pencils, ballpoint pens, sticky fingers, magnetic paper clip holders, and dust do far more damage to data on disks than such high-tech enemies as computer viruses and X-ray machines at airport security checks. In fact, it is very unlikely that X rays will do any damage at all in normal circumstances, although it is wise to avoid the repetitive exposure to X rays that can occur on extended trips with many stops, as this can result in a harmful cumulative effect similar to that which fogs photographic film. Also, X-ray machines in some countries may be poorly adjusted or generate excessive radiation, which might corrupt digitized data, creating symptoms similar to a virus infection.

 Where is your coffee cup? Are you smoking or eating popcorn, nuts, or potato chips?

Smokers on average suffer more data processing problems than nonsmokers because the ash from cigarettes, pipes, and cigars causes a significant increase in the quantity of particles in the air, which can settle on both disk surfaces and electronic components.

The tars in smoke also penetrate everywhere, combining with the ash and dust to form a chemical goo that may not be bad enough to see, but has the potential to corrupt data during read and write operations.

Although the likelihood of coffee or other liquids being spilled on disks is obvious, the keyboard is the component most subjected to a dousing. The effluent generated by snacking in front of the screen can also contaminate your keyboard.

"I can tell a lot about the personal habits and diet of an operator when I clean out a keyboard," one technician bragged to me.

I was convinced recently that I might have contracted a particular virus strain because, for the first time in three years, my keyboard stopped doing exactly as it was told and began consistently missing certain letters in a way that a virus could easily be programmed to do. ViruScan gave my system a clean bill of health, so I took a screwdriver to the keyboard and tracked my problem down to an accumulation of dirt and dross that prevented some of the keys from making proper contact. Particles of popcorn seemed to be the main contaminant!

It is not very difficult to take most keyboards apart. Disconnect the keyboard from the system, turn it over, and remove the screws. (Warning: this will almost certainly void any warranty on your computer.) Gently separate the two halves of the outer plastic casing to gain access to the keys and internal electronic circuits. Debris can be removed from the keys and circuits by blowing it away with compressed air, gently sucking it up with a vacuum cleaner, or brushing it off. I cleaned up the inside of my keyboard with a miniature, battery-powered vacuum cleaner and a very soft cosmetic brush that cost about a dollar in the local drug store. Now I regularly use the brush and vacuum to clean the keyboard from the outside in order to catch debris before it drops between the keys. This is simple preventive medicine for a portable computer, which is probably more likely to pick up foreign matter but has a keyboard that is difficult—even impossible—for the user to disassemble for cleaning.

The mouse, an increasingly popular accessory that has spread way beyond its original Macintosh environment, has software programming that provides an intriguing target for a virus creator. But if your mouse starts misbehaving, a virus is not the most likely culprit. After rolling several miles around the pad on a desk, a mouse will pick up enough dirt and other contaminants to seize up its simple mechanical system. Periodically dis-assemble and clean your mouse for smooth, reliable performance.

Is sunlight streaming through a nearby window?

If sunlight is hitting disks that you have left lying on your desk, they can quickly warp or expand enough to give read-write problems that might be confused with viral activity. It takes surprisingly little exposure to heat to render a disk useless.

Warping, which prevents the disk from spinning within its casing, is only the most obvious consequence. Even if a disk looks fine and can be loaded and run on your system, expansion from heat can physically change the location of information on it—and with 10 bytes packed into every 0.001 square inch of disk surface, it does not require much movement to effectively scramble the data stored there.

Some of the most inexplicable viral-like misbehavior on a system can be attributed to another kind of hardware heat damage. Leaving papers lying over the air vents on the top of a Mac, or allowing a PC, Amiga, or Commodore to become too hot can cause an amazing variety of problems that defy many of the conventional diagnostic tests for mal-functioning hardware.

Although the basic Macs do not have fan ventilation, they can cope remarkably well with hot environments, while some PCs, despite their forced fan cooling, can be very vulnerable. Many cooling problems arise from the addition of expansion boards and other circuitry to PC systems. Soon the inside of the case starts to fill up with extra components, all generating heat, increasing the load on the power supply, and restricting the flow of air.

Higher temperatures mean faster deterioration of the components, so chips may start to perform erratically and intermittent thermal wipeout malfunctions may arise. Even without excessive heat, the varying temperatures inside the computer casing sometimes cause expansions and contractions that can actually work the chips sufficiently loose to create all kinds of strange symptoms. It is always worthwhile to check that the chips are seated properly in their sockets. Be sure to ground any static electricity that may be in your body by touching the cabinet casing, or some other earth point, to safely discharge the static, before touching the actual surface of a chip.

It's amazing how often things can work loose inside a computer, but it takes no technical skill to remove the casing and make sure that the chips are all well seated and the plug connections sound. Well, I should modify that statement to say it takes no skill to open up an IBM PC or clone to check connections, but the Mac casing is a far more challenging proposition. It has been deliberately designed to make access difficult and so reduce the prospect of tampering.

Some of the Mac user groups that have been formed in many areas offer worthwhile introductory courses for new Mac owners that include the necessary tips on how to get into your machine. I attended such a session at the world's largest Mac user group, BMUG in Berkeley, California, and it was a revelation to see how their case poppers,

VIRUS FACT

Your most important assets after a virus infection are backups of your data and program files, kept separately and write-protected, and at least two write-protected backup copies of your operating system program.

homemade from old door hinges, made easy the miserable task of trying to access the interior of a Mac. You should not even get to the point of prying the case open unless you have the special Trox screwdriver necessary to remove the casing screws, including the two lurking under the handle and the one hidden in the battery compartment.

Once inside the Mac or the PC, and guided by a good manual, it is possible for even the novice working slowly and carefully to track down some of the causes of malfunctions. Two of the best manuals for this purpose are *Chilton's Guide to Macintosh Repair and Maintenance* by Gene W. Williams and *SAMS IBM PC Troubleshooting & Repair Guide* by Robert C. Brenner. There are also Chilton guides to the Apple Series II, IBM PC, the Kaypro, and other small computers. Diagnosis and repair disks can be invaluable aids, and with the help of those or the manuals you can tackle many problems. Most computers also have self-testing procedures as part of their operating systems. These usually run automatically when the computer is switched on.

Many overheating problems can be fixed by just looking around the computer's immediate environment and taking measures to reduce its heat load. Ensure that air can circulate freely around, in, and out of the casing and that there is not a lamp, sunlight, output from a heater, or other source creating or aggravating a cooling problem. Sometimes using a fan to increase the air flow around the system may be all that is required.

 Is the refrigerator, electric heater, washing machine, or air conditioner on the same electrical circuit as your system? Are your cables neatly coiled together? Have you a comfortable carpet on the floor?

You should consider all of these questions if your computer is misbehaving, including giving you garbled output normally associated with viral activity or software bugs. If a diagnostic program reveals no hardware fault, the problem is not necessarily with the equipment, but with the varying quality of the power coming into it. "Dirty power," or power that varies beyond the normal voltage range or contains interference, can be as bad as dirty disks. Every system should be run from a surge protector to insulate it from extreme fluctuations in the power supply.

Spikes of increased voltage, brown outs when voltages drop, sudden surges from static electricity, or lightning strikes can all damage data or result in strange malfunctions. These variations and electromagnetic interference are sometimes called *noise interference*, or *power transients*, and can be caused by a host of influences. The power company may not be able to sustain a sufficiently clean supply of electricity into your premises, and even if it does, noise interference may be created by appliances within the building that are not necessarily on the same circuit. Wires running close to each other can transmit noise interference between them, while just coiling a wire can create all kinds of unpredictable fields of electrical and magnetic energy which may adversely affect your system.

Moving one of your peripherals, such as the printer, may suddenly cause problems because the computer is picking up interference from it. Moving the system can bring it into an area of dirty power or interference—as well as possibly loosening a chip, disturbing a disk drive, or causing a connection to be no longer perfect. Always check connections first if you have a malfunction, and make it a rule to tighten up the screws that hold plugs securely in their sockets.

A rough-and-ready way of checking for interference is to move a small portable radio around the proximity of your computer and listen to it to see if it picks up interference that could be affecting your data processing. You need to tune the radio to a weak station and try several wavelengths.

You may suddenly get a problem when the humidity changes, or a cable is moved. You may be the problem yourself, walking across a wool carpet in polyester or cotton clothes, building up static electricity in your body, and then zapping 10,000 volts into your system when you touch it.

The causes and symptoms of computer malfunctions from power sources are many. You don't need to know them as long as you remember that dirty power and noise should be suspected as causes of strange computing behavior.

≈ Software Glitches

The strangest computing behavior of all—with the exception of that caused by virus or worm attacks—results from software bugs. Unfortunately they will always be a fact of computing life because of the human factor involved in creating programs.

Even the major manufacturers cannot produce perfect software and hardware combinations. As an example, in early 1990 some models of IBM's Personal Systems/2 destroyed files while running Microsoft's Windows/386. Some of the victims thought they were under a virus attack, but in fact the problem arose from obscure program instructions and required both a hardware fix and a software patch.

Just like viruses, software bugs can cause many aggravating problems, such as freezing up your keyboard, turning everything on the screen to garbage, zapping your data into eternity, and so on. If you want to learn more about bugs, read Boris Beizer's informative and entertaining *The Frozen Keyboard, Living with Bad Software,* by Boris Beizer, published by TAB Professional Reference Books.

To minimize software bug problems, stick to reputable, proven programs. If they crash or misbehave, first consult both the program manual and the information in the README file on the original disks. If those don't yield any answers, get on the phone to the software publisher's customer support service for advice.

Sometimes you have to live with bugs in programs that are so useful that you can't function without them. Life gets easier if you try to accommodate the quirks and weaknesses of tender software, just as you shift up a bit sooner in the old Chevy that jumps out of second gear when you overrev or learn how to accommodate the idiosyncrasies of an aging toaster. One tactic that often succeeds is not to let your files get too big. Very large files activate some bugs to cause data indigestion.

VIRUS · FACT ·

A utility program with the claimed ability to repair virus damage, and retrieve "lost" files can be dangerous if not used properly. Be sure to read the manuals that accompany them.

With both software bugs and hardware malfunctions, diagnosis means going through a slow, methodical process of reviewing all the things that could go wrong, your actions when the problem arose, and any changes made since the system last functioned properly. Keeping a data diary can be a real boon in getting to the heart of a problem. A record of your computing activities can be useful in many respects, as it helps identify vulnerability to virus infection and the areas in which preventive measures need to be taken, and provides information that can help in the recovery process.

Computers process information, yet many systems generate hardly any information about how they themselves are being used. Keeping computing diaries is an effective way of filling this information gap. The sample diaries shown here can get you started. The diary shown with the diskette logos is for recording software activities, and the one with the computer and keyboard logos is for information concerning hardware.

Photocopy or scan these weekly log sheets into your system and use them as they are, or modify them to your particular needs. You may, for example, prefer to combine them into one log sheet, or add columns for particular information. Or, you may want to change the headings so that your computer diary complies with other record-keeping practices you or your organization follow.

When data diaries are used as personal or business management tools, you also gain information that can help to make your computing more cost efficient. Even after only a week or two, you gain a picture of how often different applications programs are being used, which on-line services are accessed most frequently, the usage and reliability of hardware, and much more.

Such information can be applied in many ways. For example, once you determine which applications and data are most often needed, you can organize your hard disk so that these are accessed the fastest. You may also see patterns developing that could indicate the best approach to take when establishing data protection procedures.

If you manage a computer operation, instruct each operator to maintain these diaries to reinforce the use of safe computing practices. Information from these diaries also creates a picture of how effectively both hardware and software are being used and provides a guide to planning networks, scheduling the use of facilities such as a printer, and making new or replacement purchases.

System usage

SUNDAY

☐

MONDAY

☐

TUESDAY

☐

WEDNESDAY

☐

THURSDAY

☐

FRIDAY

☐

SATURDAY

☐

Data record

SUNDAY

☐

MONDAY

☐

TUESDAY

☐

WEDNESDAY

☐

THURSDAY

☐

FRIDAY

☐

SATURDAY

☐

CHAPTER

6

What to Do If You Think You Have a Virus

The information presented in this chapter is your ready reference to all the main points about computer viruses you may ever need to know. Think of this section of the book as a random access database. Imagine you are using the buttons on a touch-tone phone to get direct access to the information you need to minimize your risk of infection, or diagnose and treat a virus attack.

The Main Menu shown on the next page is your guide to accessing the information in this chapter. It resembles the menus you find in many user-friendly computer programs. To find the information you need, choose a menu selection number from 1–5, then go directly to the corresponding heading in this chapter. Or, browse through this tree of computer virus information as you wish. You can work your own way through this database in the sequence you prefer, although within each section you will find the information laid out in a progressive sequence of decisions and actions you should take, like a flow chart.

You can detach these pages from the book and put them onto a notice board or into a folder at your work station for immediate access in the event of an emergency. If you are responsible for data security and protection in an organization with many work stations, you can place a copy of these pages at each keyboard. Just remember that this material is protected by copyright. If you want to make copies for other than your own personal use, please contact SYBEX for details of reproduction rights.

```
┌─────────────────────────────────────────────────────┐
│  ┌────────────────────────────────────────────────┐ │
│  │                  MAIN MENU                      │ │
│  │                                                 │ │
│  │  1.  HELP!                                      │ │
│  │      I think I have a virus infection.  What    │ │
│  │      do I do?                                   │ │
│  │                                                 │ │
│  │  2.  BRIEFING                                   │ │
│  │      A background briefing on viruses           │ │
│  │                                                 │ │
│  │  3.  DIAGNOSIS                                  │ │
│  │      How to identify the main virus types       │ │
│  │                                                 │ │
│  │  4.  RECOVERY                                   │ │
│  │      Tips on getting rid of virus infections    │ │
│  │                                                 │ │
│  │  5.  PREVENTION                                 │ │
│  │      How to reduce your risk of virus infection │ │
│  │      by 95 percent                              │ │
│  └────────────────────────────────────────────────┘ │
└─────────────────────────────────────────────────────┘
```

≈ 1. HELP! I Think I Have a Virus Infection. What Do I Do?

Don't panic. Keep calm. It may be a false alarm. Now follow these steps:

1. Switch off your computer unless you *must* save your current work. The situation cannot get any worse while your computer is not running. Or save your current work to diskette if you can, then switch off your computer.

2. Put *all* the diskettes you have used this work session in an envelope labeled "Possibly Virus Infected."

3. While your memory is fresh, write down a brief description of the symptoms that caused you to suspect a virus infection. Then answer the following questions. If there are any yes answers, elaborate with whatever details you can recall. You may not be able to answer some questions at this stage. We'll get to those later.

Did loading programs take more time than usual?

Yes ☐   No ☐

Details:

Did other disk accesses take more time than usual?

Yes ☐   No ☐

Details:

Was there unusual screen activity?

Yes ☐   No ☐

Details:

Any hardware malfunctions?

Yes ☐   No ☐

Details:

Any files disappear?

Yes ☐   No ☐

Details:

Any strange files appear?

Yes ☐   No ☐

Details:

Any warning messages appear?

Yes ☐   No ☐

Details:

Did drive lights come on without reason?

Yes ☐   No ☐

Details:

Was memory or disk space reduced?

Yes ☐   No ☐

Details:

Were there increases in program size?

Yes ☐   No ☐

Details:

Did the size of executable files change?

Yes ☐   No ☐

Details:

4. List any files you have accessed recently via network or modem, any strange diskettes used in your system, the name of anybody else who has used your system recently, any diskettes you have used on another system and then run on this one, or any other circumstances when an infection might have been introduced.

Diskettes used:

Network access:

Different user:

5. Phone your MIS manager, network administrator, consultant, hacker friend, or whoever you (or your organization) has designated as your data processing emergency contact or other source of computer expertise. Write the name and number of this person in here *now*:

Describe to your expert the symptoms you listed in step 4. Follow the advice or instructions you are given.

Perhaps you are on your own in this data processing emergency situation and cannot readily obtain outside help. You now have two options:

- Wait until expert help becomes available. This should be your first choice unless you either feel really confident in your abilities or you will not suffer greatly if you lose the data stored on your hard disk.

- Continue through this checklist and try to identify and remove the virus yourself, if there is one. Before making the decision to power up and continue, consider the following points:

  - Does the information gathered in step 4 indicate that the probability of a virus infection is high? Have you checked for hardware problems or software bugs? (See Chapter 5.)

  - Even if there is a virus in the system, it may not yet have affected important data. Can you afford the risk of losing that data if you make a mistake when trying to eradicate the virus?

  - Can you risk losing both data and applications programs because you have good backups?

- Do you have an effective virus diagnosis and/or catching program available, or can you get one?

- Do you have sufficient computing expertise to take the chance of going on from this point without expert assistance, and so risk losing more data than may already have been destroyed?

If you decide to go ahead, follow these steps. Before you begin, have the manual for your application programs at hand. You will need it to compare the original details of the programs, such as size, title, copyright notice, and so on, with what appears on your monitor screen to check for changes made by a virus.

6. Isolate your system from any network connections. Be careful—incorrectly disconnecting the line leading into the network may cause problems on some systems.

Remember that you may be infected by a boot sector virus, which activates immediately when the system is switched on. So you next need to install DOS from a known clean source, the original diskette, that is protected by the write-protect adhesive tabs. Only physical write-protection is adequate; just labeling these files read-only won't protect them from a virus program. On 3½" DOS disks, move the notch into the protect position. Follow these steps to install DOS:

7. If you have a floppy-disk drive, put a write-protected copy of an original DOS system diskette into drive A. By having a clean DOS disk in drive A, you will bypass the automatic loading of DOS from your hard disk, which may be infected. If you have only floppy-disk drives, any boot sector viruses should now be confined to the isolation envelope you created earlier.

8. Switch on and boot up your computer, watching for any departures from normal activity. DOS will start to check your system, displaying title, copyright, and other details, and automatically noting the date and time or prompting you to insert them. Any different activity from the usual could indicate an infection.

The next step is for those with access to an antiviral program, such as ViruScan, which is on the disk that accompanies this book. If you are without an effective antiviral program or expert advice, go now to the section "3. DIAGNOSIS—How to Identify the Main Virus Types" and look for any of the symptoms listed before, then return to step 10 in this section. For example, you'll be checking that the title and copyright screens of the applications program are normal, and that the size of the program (the number of bytes listed) is the same as in the publisher's specifications. If the size is bigger than it should be, this is a sign of a probable virus infection.

9. Run an antiviral program, and follow the instructions carefully. If you are using ViruScan, the program is on a write-protected floppy to avoid any risk of it becoming infected itself. Place it in one of your drives and type

   SCAN C:

   to begin checking for virus activity on your hard disk, if you have one.

If ViruScan finds a virus, the name of the infected file and the name of the virus type will be displayed. You can then telephone the suppliers, InterPath, at (408) 988-3832 for specific instructions and to obtain a disinfection program, if one is required.

If your antiviral program indicates a boot-sector infection (or if the symptoms displayed suggest so), try to get rid of it by using the SYS command. When you use the SYS command, you replace the infected DOS program on your hard disk with the clean DOS program on the uncontaminated disk in drive A.

10. Type the command **SYS C:** at the A> prompt. If the transfer has been completed smoothly, you will get the response

    system transferred

    Repeat this process on any infected bootable diskettes because these will contain DOS system commands. It is better to back up only the data and then destroy all suspect disks. If the

SYS command fails to clear a boot sector infection and you still want to persevere on your own, then try to back up all your data files before carrying out the next step—reformatting the hard disk.

11. To reformat your hard disk, refer to your DOS manual and follow carefully the procedure outlined there.

It is psychologically very difficult to reformat a hard disk and then have to reinstall all the data files from backups and the application programs from their original disks. However, the alternative may be much worse if a virus infection is not completely eradicated and it comes back later to cause more damage. Only by reformatting and taking proper precautions as you restore your files can you trust your hard disk.

To sum up, if your computer gets infected, and you are not yourself knowledgeable about viruses, do not delay seeking expert advice if you have observed any of the following indications of virus infection:

- Program loads and disk accesses take excessively long.
- Memory and disk space are suddenly reduced.
- Unusual error messages or screen displays appear.
- Files disappear and/or strange files appear.
- Changes occur in the size of executable files.
- Drive lights come on for no reason.

Another very important emergency action to take when you know you have sustained a virus infection is to contact and warn anyone with a system that could be exposed to the same infection—for example, someone with whom you have recently networked or exchanged disks. You may help your contacts to prevent loss of their data, and they may be able to help you in your emergency if they are tackling similar problems.

≈ 2. BRIEFING—A Background Briefing on Viruses

Computer viruses are simply computer programs or sections of code that are self-replicating. Viruses attach themselves to programs and may remain concealed until the time they are set to activate. Some destroy or alter data files and other programs. Some are humorous and some are innocuous. Others may be catastrophic. They may, for example, erase everything on a hard disk. Some viruses seize up a system by reproducing so much that they consume all the memory. Viruses do not damage computer hardware except in very rare cases.

How Viruses Spread

Computer viruses can multiply and spread from one computer to another by means of infected disks, links to a network, or downloaded programs from a bulletin board. Receiving a diskette from a friend or allowing a salesperson to use a demonstration program or service personnel to run a diagnostic program on your system are all common ways that viruses get into a system. Usually the person with the infected disk does not know it has a virus on it; many viruses are spread innocently by friends and business contacts.

Viruses can move quickly from one station to another over local area networks and get into the local area file server. They spread through bulletin boards, the infecting code often being concealed in public domain or shareware software, such as useful application programs or entertaining games that you are tempted to download.

Virtually any electronic communication medium can serve as a route by which viruses spread—between machines in the same room or on opposite sides of the world.

The Main Virus Types

There are three main types of virus. Boot sector infectors attach themselves to the boot sector of hard or floppy disks containing the computer's start-up instructions. These viruses overwrite the original boot-sector instructions so that they take immediate control. They tend to create bad sectors on the disk where they store the rest of their program code.

System infectors attach themselves to various parts of the computer's operating system or master control program software. The virus may infect the input/output section of the operating system coding, the command interpreter, or any other system file. System infectors can either become memory resident and stay in the computer and in control at all times, or do their dirty work and then self-destruct. They are a particular problem because they gain control of a system before a virus detection or prevention program can get into the memory to do its job.

General purpose application infectors can affect any applications program—a word processor, a spreadsheet, a database, a special purpose program, even one you have created yourself. These viruses may or may not be memory resident and may infect every time a new program is loaded or a program is copied from one disk to another, or sometimes when accessing a directory of a disk that contains other programs. General purpose application infectors are very prolific because there are so many potential hosts for them.

≈ 3. DIAGNOSIS—How to Identify the Main Virus Types

Lots of things can go wrong with computers, with most problems usually arising from software bugs or hardware malfunctions. However, when two or more troublesome virus-like symptoms appear at the same time, the odds on an infection increase, and that's when you should check your system with an antiviral program.

These are the most commonly experienced symptoms:

1. Program loads take longer than normal.

Some viruses can gain control of the start-up procedures for a system or program. When the system is booted up or an application program is loaded, these viruses will perform their activities, perhaps extending the time taken for the load to be completed by several seconds.

2. Disk accesses seem to be excessive for very simple tasks.

For example, saving a page of text usually takes about a second, but a virus extends this to two or three seconds. Watch out particularly for a slowing down in directory access and updating procedure times.

3. Unusual error messages appear.

You might get the message

Write protect error on drive A

indicating that a virus in your system is trying to access a disk to infect it. The appearance of such messages should prompt you to investigate for viral infection, especially if the messages appear frequently.

4. Access lights come on when there is no obvious reason.

If, for example, the light for one of your drives keeps flashing when you are not accessing it to load or save data, then you may well be a virus victim.

5. System memory is reduced.

Some viruses consume considerable memory. If you have been running large programs with no problems, then suddenly you get a message that says there is not enough system memory available, this could indicate a virus infection.

6. Files mysteriously disappear (or appear).

Some viruses delete files, either randomly or according to specific instructions. If a file has disappeared from your directory for no good reason, suspect a virus. Also check for infection if unexplainable files appear.

7. Available disk space is reduced for no good reason.

This is a common warning sign that a virus has moved in and begun replicating.

8. Executable programs change size.

Normally these programs remain the same size, but if there has been a virus infection, they may get bigger, and the listed number of bytes probably would increase. Some ingenious viruses increase the size of the program, but return the number displayed back to the original specification.

9. Icons change in appearance.

Making subtle changes to the familiar Macintosh icons, such as giving the document icons a dog-eared look, is irresistible to some virus creators. Similar symptoms may appear in other systems using graphics oriented interfaces.

Hardware malfunctions and software bugs can also cause virus-like symptoms and so make diagnosis confusing. Refer to the section "1. HELP! I Think I Have a Virus Infection. What Do I Do?" in this chapter and your records of recent computing activity to evaluate if you are likely to have been exposed to an infection. If the chances are slim, go to Chapter 5 for details of bugs and malfunctions that might be confused with virus action.

≈ 4. RECOVERY—Tips on Getting Rid of Virus Infections

Removing a virus infection can be difficult and, unless you are reasonably knowledgeable about how computers function, should not be attempted without expert help.

The steps to take depend on the type of virus involved. If you think you have an infection but do not know what type of virus is in your system, you should return to the section "3. DIAGNOSIS—How to Identify the Main Virus Types" for help in making a diagnosis, or to the section "2. BRIEFING—A Background Briefing on Viruses" for descriptions of the main types of viruses.

Removing Boot Sector Viruses

Removing boot sector viruses can be very difficult. It is best to get technical help. If such help is not available, follow these instructions very carefully.

Remember that a boot sector virus attaches itself to instructions in the disk sector, which are loaded into memory immediately when the system is powered on. To remove this type of virus you must reverse the infection process, kicking the virus out and reinstalling the original boot sector coding. To do this, use the DOS utility called the SYS command and follow the instructions in your DOS manual and in step 10 of the section "1. HELP! I Think I Have a Virus Infection. What Do I Do?"

The SYS command may not always remove the boot sector virus, so you may need to use a program specifically designed for this task, some of which are public domain programs available from bulletin boards. One such program is called MDISK and can be downloaded from the Computer Virus Industry Association bulletin board. The bulletin board's phone number is (408) 988-4004.

Removing Operating System Viruses

Operating system viruses infect one or more programs within the operating system, so you must identify which files are infected.

1. Switch off your system. When you turn on the computer again, boot the system from a clean, write-protected operating system master diskette.

2. To identify the infected file or files, run an efficient virus scanning program such as ViruScan—the one included with this book.

3. Once you have identified the infected file, get the original write-protected operating system master diskette. Copy the originals of the infected files to the hard disk to eliminate the virus code by writing over it.

Ensure that the master diskette remains write-protected at all times and that you copy from that diskette to the hard disk, and not in the other direction.

Removing Application Program Viruses

Application program viruses affect any kind of application program. Follow these steps to get rid of one of these viruses:

1. Power down your system. When you switch on again, boot from a clean, write-protected operating system master diskette.

2. Use a virus scanning utility program to scan the files for these programs (they usually end with the extensions .EXE or .COM) and identify which have been infected.

3. Delete each of these infected files from the system by using the DOS DEL command: type **DEL**, then a space followed by the name of the infected file.

4. Get out your original documentation and disks for the applications program. Use them to repeat the installation procedure so that the infected files are replaced by the original noninfected versions.

≈ 5. PREVENTION—How to Reduce Your Risk of Virus Infection by 95 Percent

There are four main ways to minimize the risk of being infected by a virus:

1. Use detection utilities, virus scanning programs that will determine if an infection exists.

2. Use infection prevention programs to achieve at least some measure of protection against viruses penetrating a system.

3. Use identification and removal utilities to identify what type of virus has caused an infection and provide help in removing it.

4. Follow the "Ten Golden Rules of Safe Computing" presented at the end of this section.

Detection products work in either of two ways. The first type creates a "snapshot" of the system, recording details of the sizes of the boot sector, the operating system files, and all the executable programs. This information is stored in a log file as the "snapshot," or standard, for a clean system. When the second stage of this type of detection program is run, it checks the current state of the system against the standard in the log file. If any differences appear, then a virus infection may exist. For example, some of the executable files may have grown in size because virus coding has been attached to them. The second type of detection product is called a *vaccine* program. Vaccine programs actually go into your application programs and run a self-check, so that every time you use your word processor or spreadsheet, for example, it will be checked for possible infection. A message is displayed if a virus is present.

Infection prevention products work by monitoring your system, watching for typical actions of virus programs. For example, most viruses attach themselves to other segments of the system, like disk boot sectors, in order to replicate. The filter type of antiviral programs activate when they identify characteristic virus activity. For example, one such program might stop a virus from accessing an executable file. A warning message is also displayed on the monitor.

The identification and removal type of antiviral product minimizes your risk by first identifying characteristic virus activity, then removing the code responsible. These programs scan the entire system, looking for viruses. If one is found, a warning message appears on the screen identifying what type of virus it is, where in the system it is located, and what specific disinfectant is needed. Of course, new viruses are being created and existing ones are modified all the time, so these programs cannot always work against new strains that disguise themselves effectively.

The next section presents the Ten Golden Rules for Safe Computing. If you follow them, you will protect yourself against most of the risks of your system becoming infected.

The Ten Golden Rules for Safe Computing

1. Never load unknown disks into your system or allow anyone else to do so unless you are certain that the disks are virus free.

2. Do not use your disks in another system unless the write-protect tab is set.

3. Do not accept programs unless you can be absolutely certain that they are virus free. Try to keep all programs on separate disks from your data.

4. Be very careful if renting computers or using desktop publishing centers that do not have stringent antiviral precautions.

5. If it is essential to exchange disks or run programs or data on strange systems, adopt an effective isolation procedure. For example, do not run potentially infected diskettes on your main system, especially if it has a hard disk. Check them out first on a nonessential isolated system, such as a laptop without a hard disk or a diskette loaded in the second drive. If running your own programs or data on strange systems, transfer them first to backup disks, use these in the other system, and destroy them when the task is completed. Do not take these disks with you and risk them being inadvertently loaded into your home or office system.

6. Do not download programs from bulletin boards or from any networks that are not well managed or are not taking precautions against viruses. If necessary ask the system operator what antivirus procedures are being followed.

7. Do not let anyone else use your computer unsupervised, especially if there is the possibility of them loading their own disks into it. Remember—infection can easily be spread by the friendliest of hands!

8. Watch for unexplained changes in the way your system functions—for example, disk drives running for no good reason.

9. Use write-protect tabs extensively and create volume labels to record the size of your programs. Whenever you run the

programs, check the volumes regularly for unexplained activity that could indicate virus replication is taking place.

10. To protect against data loss from any cause, back up your data regularly on disks that do not contain program code. Clear any infection from all storage media and do not run backup disks without first checking if they are infected also. Almost 90 percent of organizations that experience a virus infection suffer a reinfection within a month, either from contaminated backups or because they have not properly disinfected their systems.

CHAPTER

7

Data Protection and Virus Infection Prevention

Now for the good news! This chapter gives you back the power over your computer that the maverick hackers and virus vandals are trying to take away from you.

In fact, you can reduce your exposure to virus infection by at least 90 percent. What's even better is that if you still become a victim, you have the power to recover comparatively painlessly and minimize the damage.

The best news of all is that you can preserve the most valuable component of your entire computer system—the data—through most of the natural hazards and unnatural disasters that you are likely to encounter. These include software bugs and hardware malfunctions as well as virus attacks.

You spend a lot of money on hardware, the tangible machinery that sits on the desk, and may well be reminded of your investment in it every month as the lease or installment payments become due. And you probably spend nearly as much money, perhaps even more, on the software applications programs that turn the hardware into useful tools.

But very quickly that financial investment pales in comparison to the value of the data that your hardware and software enable you to compile. That data is unique. Your hardware—and probably your application software—are easily replaced. In the case of many computing disasters, the replacement may cost you nothing at all apart from some inconvenience, because the losses are often covered by insurance.

However, there is no store or mail-order company that will provide replacements at any price for your data, the fruits of your computing effort. Protecting your data, your most valuable computing asset, is entirely your responsibility. Fortunately, this is not very difficult, demands no special technical knowledge, and costs hardly anything.

Ideally, every computer system should be part of a disaster preparedness plan that covers most potential hazards. We will go into the details of such a plan in Chapter 10. As you may already have some precautions in place and probably have a particular immediate concern about preventing virus infections, this chapter concentrates on that aspect of protecting your data. As a bonus, reducing your exposure to viruses and their consequences can also automatically eliminate most other risks of data loss.

≈ Use Physical Safeguards to Protect Your System

The technical jargon that computing in general and viruses in particular tend to generate sometimes obscures the fundamental truth that viruses are a people problem. The first rule of virus prevention is to protect your system against the people who may expose it to infection, either deliberately or by accident.

Your automobile is threatened by people in similar ways. Even when it is standing still, other people may damage it by deliberately vandalizing it or by accidentally running into it, or deny its use to you completely by stealing it. If you are concerned about these risks, you lock up your auto and try to park in places where these risks are minimized. You take particular care of any valuables in it by either taking them with you, or at least putting them out of sight in the trunk.

Similarly, the first line of defense for your computer system and for the data it contains consists of the physical safeguards you take to insulate it from potentially harmful human contacts. Identify these people carefully—your biggest risks may be your best friends, most trusted employees, or your own family members. Also guard your disks religiously—they are the most common source of virus infection.

Restrict Access to Your System

Anyone with access to your system—either physically, electronically via telephone or network connections, or by giving you disks—presents a potential hazard. Examine all the ways that infection may get in, and take the appropriate precautions. Try to break into your system yourself to identify the weak points, or if you are responsible for a corporate system, organize a simulated attack. A number of companies have learned a great deal about all aspects of their computer security by using "Tiger Teams," modeled on military units, to invade their own systems.

Restricting access can be as simple as keeping your system in a locked office, room, or cupboard, depending on the circumstances. There is no way that your system will contract a virus infection or have its data corrupted unless someone has the opportunity to run an infected program on it.

Physical security should also extend to all your disks or other storage media—for instance, tapes or a portable hard drive. If putting the entire system under lock and key is not practicable, there are hardware accessories available that prevent anyone from switching on the computer, and software programs that prevent unauthorized use, perhaps by requiring passwords to access files. But remember that some of the worst viruses activate the moment the computer boots up, so even an elaborate password system might not prevent an infected disk from introducing a virus into your system.

Only allow your system to be used by those who really need to use it—and then under supervision, with safe computing practices followed at all times. Allowing unrestricted access to your computer inevitably increases the risk of an infection being introduced. The PC or laptop in the den at home that the family uses as freely as the microwave or the VCR can—and has—spread viruses from those circulating in school and university systems to vital corporate systems.

Kids can forget all your warnings and one day load onto the family PC a disk containing a game or a homework project that has contracted a virus from a system at school or one at a friend's house. The virus transfers immediately to the hard disk or to a disk in another drive, or waits in RAM. This home computer may be used only occasionally for business, but once is enough for the virus to transfer to a disk brought home from the office. That disk subsequently loaded into a system linked to a network can affect hundreds—even thousands—of business computers long before any symptoms appear. Indeed, the virus may be programmed to remain hidden until it has reached a corporate network. It might be activated by such cues as the names of certain corporations appearing in a word processed document or accounting spreadsheet.

Sensible companies now encourage their employees to practice safe computing as conscientiously on their home systems as they do with their more sophisticated facilities at work. Some regard the home systems of their employees as gateways to corporate systems that need to be protected just as much as those in the office.

You also expose your system to infection when you allow software salespeople, consultants, or other outsiders access to your computer to run demonstrations or carry out tasks. If you cannot eliminate this kind of physical access to your system, at least limit it as much as possible and, when unavoidable, you might consider having outsiders check their disks at the door, just as cowboys turned over their guns before entering a saloon. You want to avoid any risk of "electronic violence" in your computing environment, and a virus is very much like a loaded gun that can go off either deliberately or accidentally.

Severely restricting physical access by employees is obviously difficult in most working situations. Employees who do not actually need to use a computer for their job functions should not be permitted to do so. The lunchtime game sessions and that new polluter (in more ways than one) of the office environment, the pornographic computer game, are often sources of virus infections.

Remember that all employees who have access to a sensitive system could also sabotage that system if they were so inclined. Many companies now move quickly to isolate from the computer system disgruntled employees who have been fired. But bear in mind that by the time such action is taken, a damaging virus may already have been placed in the system. Careful checking for infection may be advisable in any circumstances when the organization's exposure to revenge is heightened, such as during a union dispute.

Keeping a log of computer activity emphasizes to employees the need for security and can yield valuable information in the event of an infection. However, a log or diary alone (like those for hardware and software in Chapter 5) will not guard against unauthorized access. The automatic logging on and off procedures that can be created for any system can be extended to record activity with any applications programs used on the system. These procedures can be in the form of a simple batch file. *PC Magazine* has some examples available on its PC MagNet bulletin board. Don't store such logs only in electronic form, which could be lost in the event of a virus infection; make hard copies also.

When *PC Magazine* made an extensive evaluation of antiviral software for a cover story, it tested the products against live viruses. As the evaluations were being made, testers took precautions that both underline the point already made about restricting physical access, and lead us on to our next concern—controlling disks.

"Evaluators of the protection programs were instructed to work behind closed doors in a special section of PC Labs and not to let any unauthorized person in (floppy disks have a way of disappearing when crowds of people walk by)," wrote associate editor Donald P. Willmott.

Additionally, all the disks containing viruses used in the research were kept locked in a red box. It is just as important in any computing environment to keep uninfected disks physically secure to prevent unauthorized use, which might lead to a virus infection.

Guard Your Disks—and Keep the Aliens Out

Contaminated disks probably cause most virus infections. Obviously alien disks should not be run until they have been checked, but disks already being used in a clean system can easily become infected without anyone realizing it. They may, for example, be taken away and used on another system within the office, or at home—the distance of the journey not being at all proportionate to the risk of becoming infected.

You might take a disk across the room or down the hallway to process your data on a shared laser printer or plotter and it becomes infected there. You might take it home to finish a project during the weekend on your personal system, where it is exposed to infection from many sources. You may move the disk only a few feet across the desk and back again when you want to transfer data or a program from your desktop to your portable laptop, and even that short journey from one slot to another can prove hazardous.

Never lend your program disks to someone else—they may pick up an infection and bring it back to your system. If you have a legitimate reason for loaning a program, make a copy of the disk and either destroy or format it on its return.

These and many other instances of physical disk transfer from your system to another yield opportunities for infection to spread, but virtually all are circumstances under your control in which you can dictate that sensible precautions are followed. Keeping alien disks from entering your computing environment until they are demonstrably virus-free is more difficult. Those dangerous disks may enter your system in the most unthreatening manner.

Obviously you should allow no one to bring their own program disks to use on your system. Nor should you accept gifts or loans of other programs, especially pirated copies of proprietary software. Sometimes pirated copies are passed on to such an extent that they may have been exposed to a succession of systems by the time they reach you, any one of which might have been infected.

Be particularly careful of dealers who entice you with offers to load the hard disk on your new computer, or to provide floppy-disk copies of an assortment of "free" software. This may be legitimate public domain freeware, or copyrighted shareware that you are at least morally bound to license and pay a fee for if you decide to use it regularly, or it may be a pirated rip-off of proprietary commercial software. Regardless of the source of such programs, they must be suspect as far as the risk of virus exposure is concerned.

**VIRUS
FACT**

Some utility programs are able to check the status of programs and disks very easily. It makes sense to use these programs regularly and so establish a safe computing routine that can pay big dividends.

Cautious companies and some private computer users are even putting original, shrink-wrapped proprietary software disks that they have purchased through virus checks or into some form of quarantine before they use them. Such preventive precautions have become necessary because of both the deliberate and accidental infection that is ocurring in commercial software, even in well-known leading brands.

Some software retailers are unknowingly creating new virus victims because of their generous return and exchange policies. If you buy a program and do not like it, or feel that it is defective in any way, many companies allow you to return it for refund or exchange. That policy was very much in the consumer's interest until the virus epidemic began. Now it creates opportunities for viruses to be introduced, either deliberately or accidentally, into the software that is returned. An infected returned product may be resold to another customer, so never buy software that is not in its original sealed packaging. However, even this is no complete guarantee that the software you buy is virus free because some manufacturers repackage and reseal returned disks and distribute them again. Hopefully this is a practice that will fall into decline, at least among the responsible software publishers with reputations to protect. It has become as undesirable as reselling returned underwear or toothbrushes!

Where practical, and when it suits your application needs, get the latest release of a well-proven program. A reputable software publisher will continually be improving its products and so, say, release 3 of version 2 (usually expressed as 2.3) should harbor fewer unwelcome bugs of all kinds than previous versions.

Viruses will continue to infect proprietary software, but the main publishers are now taking elaborate precautions to make the risk as small as possible, certainly much less than from pirated programs, shareware, or public domain software. Software manufacturers know that they might be exposed to all kinds of legal liabilities if it could be claimed that they have disseminated a virus in a wrapped, original program. But do not expect to see "guaranteed virus free" labels on packaging, even for products that almost certainly are as clean as possible.

≈ Some Virus Prevention Techniques

If you do run an alien disk that might be infected—especially a new program—and you do not have effective virus detection software, at least try first to open it as read-only data files in a word processor. Look to see if there are unusual or rude messages among what will be largely unintelligible programming instructions. Such messages are a feature of many viruses, and you might want to take the time to do a search for such key words as "warning," "virus," "ha-ha," plus some of the more common four-letter expletives. Verify the name, address, and copyright notice of the author or publisher. If these are absent or appear bogus, suspect hacker activity. But be warned: checking the programming by running it through a word processor may be enough in itself to release some kinds of viruses, though it is unlikely.

Another precautionary measure is to read any on-disk documentation that accompanies a new program, usually contained in the .TXT or .DOC files. A carefully-constructed Trojan Horse program delivering a virus may contain a README file to further the deception that it is an innocent piece of software, but if the phrasing or literary quality of the text in such a file is poor, this should be seen as a warning about running the program.

Write-protect tabs are great disk protectors, and you should always use them on any disk that does not need data written to it, including both program disks and disks on which you store your archives and backups. Sticking the adhesive tab over the notch on minifloppies or moving the tab on the plastic case of a microfloppy will insulate it from subsequent virus attack. If a disk is already infected, write-protecting it may seem like locking the stable door after the horse has bolted, but at least you will be warned of the possible presence of a virus in your system: If you get an unexplained write-protect error message when any protected disk is in a drive and you are not deliberately trying to access it, consider this a warning of a possible virus infection.

Always write-protect the boot disk for your operating system and use only that disk to boot up a system that has only floppy-disk drives. If you have a hard disk with the operating system on it, with the help of your DOS manual you can extend this protection even further by write-protecting your .COM and .EXE files so that they become read only. The procedure varies with different versions of DOS, and there are utility programs available to make the task easier.

If you have a hard disk, never switch on your computer with floppy disks in the drives. This is to ensure that you always boot from the hard disk and not from one of the drives, which may contain a floppy disk with a boot sector virus able to take immediate control of your system.

It makes sense periodically to replace vulnerable operating system files on your hard disk with those from the original operating system disk that you know is virus free. In addition to the .COM, .EXE, and .SYS files that are popular virus targets, don't forget the mouse and other device drivers that are loaded from CONFIG.SYS. Replace those regularly also.

≈ Be Particularly Careful When Using Bulletin Boards

Because their very purpose is to act as communications media for the exchange of data and often for programming code as well, bulletin boards are very vulnerable as carriers of viruses. However, bulletin boards are too valuable a resource to ignore, and it is still worth using those that take appropriate precautions, including testing program files.

Although the undesirable elements on bulletin boards will try to tempt you, do not download any program from suspect bulletin boards. Stay away from boards that disseminate pirated software. You are as likely to get a computer virus from them as you are a human virus from patronizing an unsafe brothel or bathhouse.

An increasing number of users who find roaming the bulletin boards both fun and useful now do so on a computer that they keep specially for this purpose. If you do pick up a virus and identify it, you can isolate it to that system and not transfer it to your main system where it can infect valuable data files. This is a good use for an old system that has become too slow or otherwise too limiting for your main computing needs, or for your second computer if you have both a desktop and a laptop. It is especially appropriate if the second machine does not have a hard disk where a virus can lurk between sessions on bulletin boards, waiting for an opportunity to break out of its quarantine and find new victims.

The downloading of programs that have been compressed to save both space on the board's memory and online transmission time have become a particular problem. The compression and decompression processes require special programs, so these programs are good places in which both to hide viruses and have viruses activate to do the kind of damage we discussed earlier.

If you do download a program straight onto your hard disk from a bulletin board, a network, electronic mail system, or some other source, at least put it into temporary isolation before you run it and risk releasing a virus among all the data and programs on your hard disk.

The way to do this is to copy the downloaded file first onto an empty floppy disk—one that is formatted and does not have anything else on it, particularly no operating system files. Then delete from your hard disk the file that you downloaded and do not use the new program until you have tested it from the floppy disk, preferably on an isolated system without a hard disk containing valuable data that might be damaged. Only if the new program gets a clean bill of health should it be loaded onto your hard disk. If there is anything suspicious, discard the diskette containing the program. It's just not worth taking any chances.

One key to keeping power over your computer, like the key to many things in life, is having the right attitude. Collecting programs because they are attractive or cheap and hoarding disks because you do not regard them as disposable items are dangerous attitudes. Disks cost negligible amounts when compared to the value of data, so don't hesitate to destroy any that might be infected.

Some programs offered on bulletin boards or sold at computer swap meets seem to offer the moon and, like any bargain, there may be a catch. A really great program will soon become well known, and it is unlikely that its author will choose to remain anonymous. An unknown program to which the author has not attached a credible name should be suspected immediately. So also should a physically small program claiming to deliver elaborate, grand results. Any such clues should make you suspect that the program you have downloaded from a board or obtained on a disk may be a virus hidden in a Trojan Horse. In this case the best preventive action is to delete this program from your hard disk, or reformat the floppy on which it has been saved, and not take any more risks with it.

≈ Use Good Quality, Up-to-Date Antiviral Software

You may have thought this should be first on the list of virus prevention measures, but in fact much antiviral software is a mixed blessing at best, and in some situations can be downright dangerous.

Some antiviral programs are just no good. Entrepreneurs around the world have seen the virus epidemic as a great opportunity to make a fast buck, and they have offered antiviral software that runs the gamut of irresponsibility. Some software programs are ineffective because they have been rushed to market without proper development or testing, while other programs are incapable of providing the protection that their manufacturers claim they do.

Other software may be reasonably effective for a time, but if not kept up to date becomes useless in preventing infection from the large number of new virus strains that keep appearing.

At the time of writing, there are no standard criteria for evaluating antiviral software, no meaningful government or consumer association approval or rating schemes. Even computer experts have difficulty judging the efficiency of the different products without specialist virus knowledge, and some published critical reviews display surprising naiveté and ignorance.

In 1989, two of the most respected names in computing—IBM and Apple—released antiviral software packages that were relatively effective, but did not offer comprehensive protection. They were competently written, responsibly tested, and they provided effective prevention and recovery procedures against specific viruses. But if you have one of those programs for your Mac or PC, you cannot rely on it to protect you completely because new viruses are being written all the time to outwit all antiviral programs.

We have included the ViruScan antiviral sotware with this book (see Chapter 11) because it has been tested under wide-ranging conditions by a number of corporations with the necessary expertise to make valid value judgements. In addition, ViruScan can be updated easily. Other programs of similar merit may become available, and no book can anticipate them and give long-lasting valid advice on which ones to choose.

The best approach is to follow authoritative media comment and news about the virus epidemic and use up-to-date versions of well-recommended antiviral software from reputable sources. Do not rely on new product reports in magazines that run the claims in the manufacturers' media releases without properly testing new products. Virtually every antiviral software publisher, just like the manufacturer of every headache pill, claims their product is a cure-all. None are, and only a few come close to delivering on their apparent promises.

All antiviral programs—including the software that comes with this book—are potentially more dangerous than not using any antiviral software at all if they lull you into a sense of false security. If you rely completely on them and think you do not need to follow the basic safe computing principles outlined in this chapter, then you may be putting your faith into the electronic equivalent of snake oil.

You have four basic types of antiviral software from which to choose. Let's look at their distinctive characteristics and highlight some of their inherent limitations.

Prevention products are like software security gates, intended to stop viruses from entering your system. These products either prevent unusual activity or warn you that something untoward is going on so that you can decide the most appropriate response to make. They block typical virus activity by looking for the generic characteristics of a typical virus and try to stop the invasive program as soon as they recognize something suspicious. They react just as a security guard might when confronted with an intruder that behaves in a threatening way.

In addition to their generic antiviral defensive shields, some prevention products have the ability to give warnings about running any programs that have not been authorized. They are the equivalent of physical security checks for the identity of approved entrants into the system. Though these can be very effective, they can also be fooled by clever viruses hiding in authorized programs. A human factor also enters the situation if the product provides frequent false alarms—you may cease to trust it and then not respond when it finds a genuine cause to sound a warning.

Detection products offer little if any protection against a virus getting into your system, but raise the alarm and may halt all normal system activity if they find an infection. The operative word here is *if*; as with other antiviral programs, detection products are a compromise between the ideal and the practically achievable. They usually monitor your system for generic virus activity and for changes from the normal way in which your operating system and applications programs function. As more viral strains are created, and as viruses become more clever at disguising their activities and mimicking legitimate applications, both prevention and detection products risk becoming outdated and ineffective.

The third category of antiviral software is comprised of *identification products* which, after an infection has occurred, compare the symptoms to those of known viruses, tell you which strain matches those symptoms, and usually provide some help in removing the infection. Again, this type of antiviral product can become outdated very quickly, like a doctor who doesn't keep up with the medical literature.

It has become popular, for marketing purposes as well as other valid reasons, to label antiviral programs as *vaccination products*. In medical terminology, a vaccine consists of benign viruses, dead virus particles, or weakened viruses, all of which generate antibodies to combat a specific strain of viral infection. The computer virus vaccination products do not really behave in this fashion, and the label is usually applied to detection products that sound warnings if there have been changes to executable programs. As some of these programs automatically check themselves anyway, there may be conflict between the vaccination program and the executable program it seeks to protect, false alarms being a frequent consequence.

Some antiviral software concentrates on a particular approach to prevention, detection, or damage control; others combine elements of two or more basic types. The type you choose will depend on a variety of factors, for example, the degree of your concern about viruses and your exposure to risk. Everything is a compromise and, other things being equal, the most protective antiviral software will do the most intensive monitoring of your system's activity. Consequently, it is likely to slow things down more and raise a higher proportion of false alarms than less effective antiviral software.

There is no point in having software protection that gets in the way of the efficient use of the computer. If the antiviral product slows down things too much, conflicts with the application programs you need to use, or sounds too many false alarms, you may well be better off without it, at least as a regular part of your computing routine. Concentrate on the other basic, safe computing practices and you can reduce your risk of an infection to an acceptable level, especially if you have an efficient data backup policy.

Instead of overdosing on prophylactic electronic medication, if trouble does strike or is suspected, use the antiviral identification products such as ViruScan as you would a medical test—only when the circumstances justify. I keep my copy of ViruScan reassuringly close at hand, ready to use if an emergency arises.

You may already have quite powerful, if not complete, virus detection and data recovery facilities available in the form of a utility program that monitors system activity and retrieves "lost" files. But be warned that a powerful utility program can also shoot your system in the foot if not used carefully. Even experienced computer users should use them with caution, treading warily and following the procedures in the manuals. We get used to trying to fly new applications programs by the seat of our pants, ignoring the manuals if possible. That can be a risky business with powerful utilities.

≈ New Technological Developments in Virus Prevention

The best and most effective prevention of virus infection will come when computer architecture has been changed drastically to provide a computing environment in which these self-replicating programs cannot flourish. OS/2 could be a step in this direction, especially with its multitasking capabilities that make it easier to run antiviral software in the background, ready to leap into action to defend your data if viral activity is identified.

The Disk Defender, a hardware device created by Dennis Director, signifies another step in the right direction when it comes to protecting existing PC and Macintosh operating systems. Director has developed a comparatively simple hardware circuit that acts as a barrier to keep viruses out of a portion of the hard disk. This is a product slightly ahead of its time, because Disk Defender became available before the virus problem reached its current epidemic proportions and before some of the

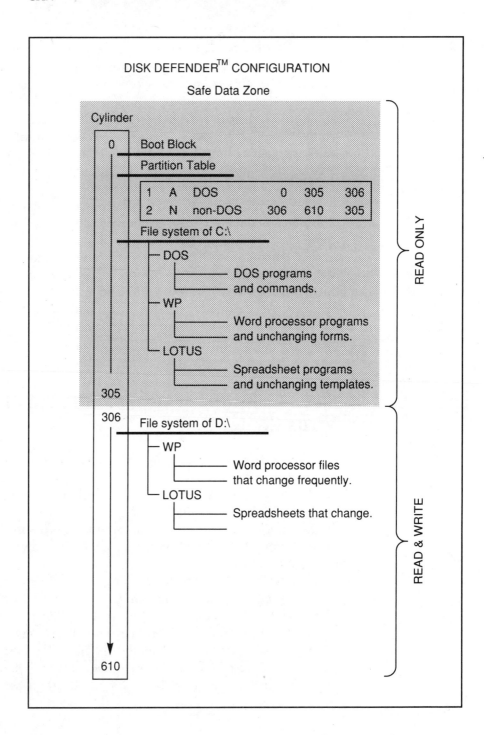

popular applications programs were sufficiently refined to function efficiently with only limited disk-writing access.

As the above diagram of Disk Defender's configuration shows, putting operating system and application program files into a read-only zone of the hard disk protects them from virus attack. Data files stored behind the hardware barrier created by Disk Defender are protected also. It is the hard disk equivalent of putting a write-protect tab over the notch in a floppy, but more flexible because part of the disk can still be written to and files on it changed.

This is an appropriate prevention route worth investigation by systems managers and users. The hardware barrier can be tailored to a variety of situations in both Mac and DOS environments. Disk Defender's designer, Dennis Director, can be reached at (708) 491-2334.

≈ The Ultimate Protection—Your Backups

Having a really effective data backup policy will not prevent a virus infection, but is still the best means of defense because it preserves the data and makes complete recovery possible. Since viruses may spread to backup copies, your backups should be on disks or tapes containing only data, and there should be two or three generations of backups retained to reduce the risk of losing all data records because you have also backed up a virus program.

If you have data that you *must* preserve, such as essential corporate records or the manuscript of a book, you must also backup electronic data storage with conventional *hard copies*, or printouts of your data. Print it onto paper in a form that can be scanned easily. Don't use fancy fonts or formatting, but create a hard copy in the typeface and with the layout that can be most accurately read by one of the many optical scanning devices now available. Store these copies securely, as described in Chapter 10. Then, if all your computerized data is lost because of a virus infection, or for any other reason, you can bring out your hard copies and either have them scanned for you or buy yourself a scanner at that point.

Most people will not need to go to such extremes, but you will need to modify traditional methods of backing up data to protect your files in view of the realities of the new virus infection risk. If you don't already have a backup routine and have not suffered a serious data loss from virus infection or any of the many other computer hazards, then you are computing on borrowed time and should not press your luck for a moment longer!

Although hard disks are inherently very reliable devices, they will all fail at some time or other, and the advent of viruses greatly increases the hazardous practice of storing your work only on the hard disk, even for short periods. Nor is storage on a single floppy secure. You need at least one duplicate record in reserve, preferably two. How you make these backups depends very much on your individual or corporate computing circumstances, budget, and dependence on your data. Whatever method you adopt, it will have little or no value if it is not convenient or practical enough to be used regularly and does not produce backups that enable you to restore your data easily if you lose it.

Most users probably have sufficient backup equipment already in their systems. The routine is simple. Save work in progress periodically to the hard disk (or to a floppy if you do not have a hard disk). You can set up many applications programs to save work at regular intervals, say once every 15 minutes, or a batch file can be written to automate the desired backup routine. But never forget that this backup may be affected by a virus just as easily as the current working copy.

At least hourly, or when you change files, make a separate back up of your work to another disk (to a floppy if your first backup is on the hard disk, or to a second floppy if you don't have a hard disk). I go braces-and-belt by making backup copies to two floppies—to a minifloppy in drive A and to a microfloppy in drive B. Then, if I get a hardware failure, the power goes off, or there is an earthquake or some other disaster and urgent work needs to be completed, I can use my backups on any PC, desktop, or portable computer. I back up really crucial data as unformatted ASCII files. This gives tremendous retrieval flexibility, including easy transfer to a Mac or other operating system.

Although the original disks—write protected, of course!—are the clean backups for your applications programs, it may pay to make additional disk backups if you put a lot of effort into configuring those applications programs to meet your specific needs. Keep these program backups separate from the data backup disks. Don't mix programming and data on the same disk.

Periodically you may want to make an archive backup of your entire hard disk. This is tedious and could take considerable time, depending on the amount of data on your disk, but you can speed things up by using a compression backup utility. Fastback Plus, PC Tools, and the Norton Backup program in the Norton Utilities collection are popular examples of such utility programs for the PC, and there are a number of choices for the Macintosh and other systems.

Clearly label and date all backup disks and keep at least one copy in a secure place away from your system.

If you want to save time and are prepared to incur more costs, then adding a second hard disk is the most convenient approach to duplicating both data and program files. The hardware can be built into your computer or hooked up externally by cable. The big snag is that the second hard disk is as vulnerable to virus infection as the first one, and so may be worthless when you really need to recover data from it.

Probably the safest backup medium is tape. The minicartridge backup systems are very fast, easy to use, and should come down steadily in price as competition increases. You can also make multiple backup copies on an ordinary Beta or VHS video recorder with special software and connecting cables. The inherent disadvantage of storing data linearly on tape is that you do not have the convenience of random access to it, but this minus can actually be a big plus in limiting the potential damage from a virus infection.

To prevent your backups from causing reinfection, they must be used cautiously during the recovery routine after a virus attack. The Computer Virus Industry Association says that nine out of ten systems are reinfected within a week, mainly because the virus has been reintroduced from an infected floppy when trying to restore data. Chairman John McAfee, after reviewing thousands of cases, says that any floppy that has been inserted into a system infected within the previous two years must be regarded as suspect.

So the disks that you are using for your backups should always be formatted with volume labels and dates, and these checked for viruses if they have to be run to restore data. Any changes you discover in checking may indicate that the backup disks also have been infected. Indeed, you should assume that your backup disks are infected and copy all the non-executable files from them to new formatted disks, which are then used to restore your hard disk.

It may seem a complicated and time-consuming nuisance to carry out these virus prevention and data protection routines, but most of them are applied common-sense procedures that really do not involve much inconvenience. And these measures have the potential for a big payoff in time and savings in cost compared to suffering an infection and not being able to restore valuable data. At any rate, these are good habits to adopt. When they become second nature, you can carry on computing without feeling paranoid about the risk of a virus infection with all its consequences.

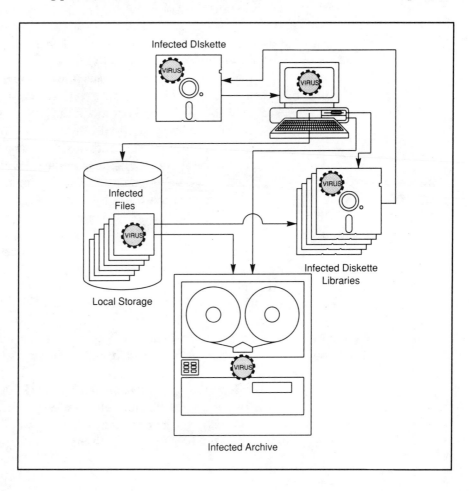

CHAPTER

8

The Rogues' Gallery of International Computer Viral Villains

There are hundreds of different computer viruses circulating around the world. Every day new versions emerge of the over 80 distinctive viral strains and derivatives that have been identified in the DOS environment alone.

The decade of the nineties opened with a sharp increase in the rate of Macintosh infections. New and more potent Macintosh viruses emerged to join the already diverse range of derivatives of existing strains in that fast-growing computing sector. The nVIR strain that first began infecting Macintoshes in West Germany in 1987 has been followed by more than 30 distinct varieties of Macintosh viruses that have spread around the world.

A virus may start out as humorous or innocuous and then have destructive capacities added to it. This is why you cannot categorize any virus as harmless with absolute certainty.

Some viruses that began as innocent pranks have developed into malevolent data destroyers. The Christmas virus created by a German student to amuse his friends ran amok in IBM's international network, affecting systems in many nations. Others timed to attack systems at the end of the century have had their fuses shortened and their destructive power increased. Viruses aimed at specific targets in Europe have ricocheted by satellite around the world to cause chaos in systems as far apart as Australia, Canada, and Japan. Strains thought to infect only one kind of file have cropped up a few days later with distinctly different characteristics as hackers have changed them to make them more effective at eluding detection.

You cannot make generalizations about viruses because these international viral villains are moving so fast on such a wide global scale. We now have thousands of people of at least 20 different nationalities, including some of the most brilliant software engineers in the world, experimenting with virus programming. They are manipulating and changing existing virus code and pushing forward with the creation of radically new types of replicating programming in a flurry of technological and intellectual activity. Out of this unique cultural, technological, and social phenomenon could come radical and beneficial new ways in which computers could serve us. Or the increasingly hostile and destructive programming aimed straight at the soft underbelly of the world's community of computer users could result in an orgy of international information processing terrorism.

Software failure already costs the United States alone over a billion dollars a year, according to the congressional report *"Bugs in the Program."* The worldwide figure could be double that, and the failure rate of software is being accelerated by the new strains of viruses that are created to deliberately sabotage software. With no comprehensive and effective antiviral defense in sight, the statistics will continue to get worse as existing strains replicate and new ones join them to fuel the spread of infection.

However disturbing the global figures, they really only strike home on an individual basis when one's own computer system crashes and your data dies. The infection of a thousand unknown systems does not have the impact of the infection of one on which your livelihood depends, or one that is processing data essential to the medical well-being of a loved one. By 1990, at least 2 million computer systems have fallen victim to viral infections, according to CVIA figures. Many of those were tragedies to varying degrees for the individuals and businesses that had their data destroyed.

> *At least 2 million computer systems have already fallen victim to viral infections ...*

Our computer-dependent society is under attack by enemies we cannot identify, whose motives we have great difficulty in understanding. The advice to "know thine enemies" cannot be followed despite the vast information-gathering power computers have given us. These enemies are many, and they act in a random, uncoordinated way using the very technology they are attacking to defy detection.

We can only be sure of what we currently know about hackers: that those who create and spread viruses are predominantly young males, ranging in age from the teens to early thirties, with above-average intelligence. They are concentrated in the industrialized Western nations, and they are generally loners who relate more easily to computerized communications than conventional human contacts. They display hostile attitudes toward the establishment as represented by the government, the military, and big business. Most of these virus creators are not motivated by greed, although it is conceivable that their skills could be exploited increasingly by those seeking to deploy the destructive power of viruses for monetary and political gain.

Apart from these broad generalizations, our computing enemies are faceless. However, we do know about the weapons they are using, even if the international arsenal of viruses keeps changing in confusing patterns of evolution and innovation.

Much of the confusion stems from the way that viruses are named. There is no respected organization like the ones that recognize new botanical specimens or medical diseases to acknowledge the discovery of a virus and assign it a name that is automatically and universally accepted. So some viruses are named several times over. Computer virus researchers tend to assume that their first encounter with a strain is a unique discovery, so they slap a name on a program that at the same time is being given another name by another researcher or contributor to bulletin board dialogs on new viral attacks.

This happens particularly with many viruses coming into the United States via satellite links from Europe. They start off with one name and acquire others as soon as they appear on the other side of the Atlantic.

Much confusion also comes from the fact that a virus that appears to be new often is not. Since it is less work for a virus creator to change a virus that has already been written than it is to write a new one, virus programmers tend to "recycle" much of the code of an existing virus and add new code only when necessary to suit their particular purpose. It may appear new to someone who encounters the modified version for the first time, so it is given a new name.

In other cases, elements of two or more viruses are merged to form a kind of hybrid program that retains the most effective characteristics of its "parent" viruses. Commercial plants and livestock are produced in a similar way by selecting parents to create genetically enhanced offspring. Such a virus may include a very efficient delivery mechanism, the best replicating code available, and programming that enables it to hide easily.

VIRUS FACT

Proprietary programs in their original sealed packaging are almost entirely safe. Although viruses have occasionally infected proprietary software programs, most publishers are taking elaborate precautions to make the risk very small, certainly much smaller than from pirated programs or from shareware or public domain software. But software manufacturers know they may be exposed to all kinds of legal liabilities if it can be claimed that they have disseminated a virus in a packaged original program. That's why you won't see "guaranteed virus free" labels on packagings, even on products that almost certainly are clean.

As there are many permutations, with often only slight differences between them, the naming of these hybrids becomes particularly difficult. No strain remains pure for long when any particular version of a virus may pass through the systems of several hackers who cannot resist the temptation to tweak it to make a piece of the programming more efficient, to polish up a routine, or add some individuality.

Like good software programming, a virus tends to evolve and mature as people modify it, but at this time it is not possible to tell when a virus has evolved to such an extent that it becomes a new program altogether and so merits a new name.

Also, a virus may start off as humorous or innocuous and then have destructive capacities added to it so that it assumes an entirely new personality, although its name stays the same. This is why you cannot categorize any virus as harmless with absolute certainty, or assume the character of a virus from the name by which it is known. If in February you say the Ping Pong virus does no harm, by March the little bouncing ball may have acquired the capacity to destroy your data and so become a distinctly different and vicious character.

To further complicate the situation, some viruses remain the same but have a different name attached to them for no apparently logical reason at all. If you think family trees get complicated, you haven't a hope of deciphering the processes by which viruses acquire their names.

Fortunately, whether they have accurate names or not, most viruses can be classified. As we have discussed earlier, virtually all viruses fall into three main classes or categories, defined by the major characteristics displayed when they infect systems:

- Boot sector infectors travel on floppy disks and gain control of operating systems by attaching to the boot sectors of disks.

- System infectors infiltrate operating system files, where they both replicate and control how the system functions.

- Generic application infectors hide in all kinds of applications programs, activating when the program is run to seek new opportunities to replicate, corrupt data, and change the behavior of the programs they infect.

Some viruses can now use all three of these methods of infecting systems.

In addition to these broad categories, certain viruses have achieved separate and distinctive notoriety because of their actions or the way they have been programmed. Descriptions of a selection of these viruses follow this section. Please remember that the viruses described may have acquired different characteristics and names by the time you read this.

There is not even universal acceptance of the definition of the term "computer virus." One leading European researcher is promoting the concept that a virus only reproduces once and so is distinguished from a worm program. I have stuck with the more commonly accepted, and what seems to me more logical, definition of a virus being simply a program that replicates itself as the prime objective in the way it was written. That distinguishes viruses from worms, the latter usually being destructive routines created to spread through systems in a planned search for specific targets, but do not have the ability to replicate themselves. If they replicate, or clone, themselves in the process—either by accident or design—they effectively become viruses.

So here is our rogues' gallery of international viral villains, a motley collection of self-replicating programs from around the world, very different in their characteristics but all with the ability to damage your data.

≈ DOS Environment Viruses

Let's start with the DOS viruses, which are the most numerous due to DOS's popularity in the computer community generally, and with hackers in particular.

The *Disk Killer* is a boot sector virus and the most destructive of the new strains to emerge in late 1989. When it activates, it displays the following message:

> **Disk Killer Version 1.0**
> **from Ogre Computers**
> **now killing disk.**
> **Please do not power**
> **down your system.**

Ten seconds before the message is displayed, Disk Killer has already initiated a low-level format of the hard disk. Powering down immediately when the warning appears on screen is not effective, as everything on the disk has been destroyed before you can react.

Disk Killer has spread rapidly and has infected proprietary software distributed by at least one leading manufacturer, which engaged in an enormously expensive recall program and took all the appropriate steps that it could to protect its customers. (Not naming the brands or product names of proprietary software that have contracted virus infections seems to be the fairest policy because the cases we know most about are those in which the manufacturer has revealed details to try to minimize the damage.) The message to glean from the Disk Killer incident, and other infections of proprietary software, is that users must not assume that any new application program is "clean." All new software entering a system should be checked for infection.

The *Dark Avenger* is a .COM and .EXE file infector that promises to be a steadily increasing problem because it is both very infectious and destructive. Dark Avenger will seek new host programs at virtually any moment of application program activity, including loading, executing, or transferring code or data between systems.

For example, if you load an infected program from a floppy to your clean hard disk, the Dark Avenger may activate immediately. Even the scanning of the infected floppy by a virus detector can activate the virus and cause an infection in the system.

The *Zerobug* is another .COM infector from Europe. It originates and destroys data both quickly and efficiently. We should be particularly concerned about Zerobug because it incorporates a new method of outwitting many of the virus detection programs now on the market.

Some detection programs rely on monitoring program size to identify hidden infections. Many viruses attach and conceal themselves within the code of application programs, inevitably increasing the size of those programs above the manufacturer's standard. The Zerobug hides in application programs, but it remains undetected by changing a program's new identification details back to the manufacturer's standard. This is one of the most ingenious and effective methods of virus concealment to have emerged so far, as it automatically renders obsolete many antiviral programs and utilities that rely entirely on checksums, snapshots, or other devices to compare the current status of a program against its original specification to seek symptoms of a virus infection.

The *Alabama* is a .COM and an .EXE file infector that also introduced a disturbing new device. Whenever files are copied or otherwise activated on an infected system, Alabama renames them, giving them the name of another existing file on the victim's system. Soon all the data file listings are scrambled—the data is still there, but you cannot access it effectively because you do not know under what file name it is stored.

Such activity by viruses can be very confusing and stressful on users, particularly those who are not comfortable working with computers. The stress factor can be considerable when this kind of aggressive, unpredictable, and apparently insolvable activity occurs when you are tired, or when a great deal of work appears to have been destroyed. It's as if someone leaned over your shoulder, pressed the Delete key, and trashed your work. Your reaction might include pain, hostility, and the desire for retaliation if that action was carried out against you by a tangible human being. The same emotions come into play when the machine you have trusted to behave logically and reliably in accordance with your instructions suddenly eats up all your data.

Such stress and other negative emotions are likely to be more severe when the attacker remains concealed and anonymous. The consequences of virus attacks—or the fear of them—on the relationships and attitudes of humans to their computers are very important, but there is still very little research data available on this important subject. The Alabama and similar viruses that stimulate anger and frustration in victims add yet another dimension to the virus issue that represents a significant management challenge.

The *Yankee Doodle* is, fortunately, an innocuous virus in its original form. It is activated by a computer's internal clock; at 5 P.M. it causes the tune "Yankee Doodle Dandy" to be played over the computer's loudspeaker. Initially, this virus did not destroy data or overload systems by replicating out of control.

The *Do Nothing* virus started as an innocuous virus that infected .COM and .EXE files without destroying data or overloading systems by repetitive replication, acting much like a gun without bullets. The fact that it did nothing other than establish itself efficiently in the .COM and .EXE files made it an attractive delivery vehicle for hacking into a malicious virus.

The *Jerusalem* or *Israeli* (and sometimes misnamed *Friday the 13th*) virus is such an efficient replicator that it soon spread rapidly after being first discovered in 1987; so far it is responsible for an estimated 60 percent or more of all PC environment infections.

At the time of writing, if your system had contracted a virus infection, the virus was most likely a strain of some version of the Jerusalem. Fortunately, because it is so widespread and has been around so long, most antiviral software will pick up at least the more common and earlier versions of the Jerusalem—any antiviral program that doesn't is not much good.

The Jerusalem premiered at the Hebrew University in Jerusalem, and soon there were reports of infections from other Israeli systems, including one in a military computer. This fueled speculation that the virus had been created by Palestinian electronic saboteurs and was triggered to go off on Friday, May 13, 1988—the anniversary of the partition of Palestine.

This virus infects both .COM and .EXE files, and the most common version still has the bug that causes it to continuously reinfect .EXE files. Consequently, the infected system is overloaded and crashes before the virus's activation date, which is any Friday that coincides with the 13th day of the month (as happens at least once in any year). In a report of just one infection in Haifa, this overloading effect was said to have destroyed 7,000 hours of work.

The *Jerusalem-C* version of this virus no longer has this bug and identifies the .EXE files that have not already been infected. So the Jerusalem-C does not run out of control and warn of its own presence by its sheer replicating activity. This refinement makes it more dangerous than the original virus because it has a longer incubation period which enables it to infect more systems.

There is also a *New Jerusalem* or *Jerusalem-D* virus that does not have the original Jerusalem's time delay. This version starts destroying data immediately and gives no advance warning of an infection.

The *Sunday* virus is another version of the Jerusalem that makes use of Jerusalem's very efficient replicating and infecting coding. As the name implies, the Sunday virus is activated when the internal clock of a system it has infected reaches Sunday. Upon activation of the virus, the operator is greeted by the following message:

Today is Sunday. Why are you working?
All work and no play make you a dull boy.

Before or during the display of the message, the Sunday virus has garbled the FAT (file allocation tables) section of the operating system so that files cannot be located. Just as the original Jerusalem has such an efficient infection mechanism that it is now by far the most widespread of all computer viruses, one can anticipate that the Sunday will rapidly spread to both private and corporate systems in all developed nations.

More bad news about the Jerusalem: we may not have experienced the worst of it yet, with even more destructive versions set to activate on various dates in the nineties. There is a theory among some virus creators that the ultimate virus will be one that secretly infects as many systems as it can before doing any damage. Its built-in time bomb would be set years ahead so that the virus has plenty of time to spread to millions of systems.

One version of the Jerusalem virus with various names, including the appropriate name *Century*, seems to fit this agenda; it is set to go off on January 1, 2000. Before the words

Welcome to the 21st Century

appear on screen, the Century virus scrambles the FAT and then writes zeros to every sector on every disk. (Some military and research establishments use this method of writing zeros to completely disinfect hard drives because it is more effective than reformatting in destroying data on magnetic storage.)

Of course, the Century virus can be hacked to change the activation date, and this has already happened. Hopefully, effective antiviral hardware and software will have been developed by the year 2000 to deactivate the original Century if it has succeeded in spreading to millions of systems.

New variants of the Jerusalem and some of the older versions that just appear to be new keep cropping up with different names attached to them. These include the *Black Hole* and the *Russian* virus. There is also a version that is activated by backup routines, a particularly dirty trick.

The *Friday the 13th* virus is often confused with the Jerusalem in naming because it also activates on any Friday that falls on the 13th day of a month. It destroys programming when activated, but it does not continue uncontrolled replicating like the Jerusalem.

The original version was first reported in South Africa in 1987, but soon was recognized in so many other countries that one cannot be sure where it originated. This virus knocks out three .COM files and then becomes inactive. Many victims first learn of its presence when the drive A light comes on after the virus infects two of the .COM files on the hard disk. By then it is too late to do anything about it.

You can expect worse if you get this polite message appearing on your monitor:

We hope we haven't inconvenienced you.

This message was put into a second-generation version of the Friday the 13th virus with the ability to infect every file in the subdirectory you are currently using, and may break lose and rampage through all your files if it gets into the directories in the system path and the root directory.

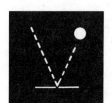

The *Ping Pong*, also known as the *Bouncing Ball, Italian,* or *Vera Cruz* virus, is a boot sector virus that keeps cropping up in many corporate systems. The dot bouncing around on the screen appears to be the only consequence of infection, but some versions have a bug that results in overwriting of the FAT in about one in every eight cases of infections, causing the system to crash and data to be lost.

Rebooting the system is usually enough to get rid of Ping Pong. The earlier versions only infected floppies, but later versions of the same strain can seriously damage hard disks also.

The *Ghost* virus that first appeared in 1990 is often confused with Ping Pong because it also features a bouncing ball on the screen. But the Ghost infects both boot sectors and the .COM files on disks and floppies. So in addition to using the SYS command to disinfect the boot sector, it is also necessary to remove all infected .COM files.

The *Columbus Day*, also known as the *October 13* or *Datacrime* virus, actually performed a service to the computing community in October 1989. It generated so much advance publicity and media hype that many people took the virus epidemic seriously for the first time. Executives and managers who read about the virus in newspapers were motivated to allocate resources to develop safer computing practices, which will probably have long-lasting benefits in protecting their systems.

There was an unprecedented flurry of international activity to find and eliminate the virus from important systems. Antiviral experts managed to save data on crucial Swiss government systems that had been infected, and data damage was either averted or minimized on infected systems at universities, national railway systems, banks, and electronics and armaments companies as far apart as France and Australia. The Royal National Institute for the Blind in London lost important records due to virus activity, but the fear that the Columbus Day virus had spread to the thousands of computers used by blind people proved groundless. Indeed, the infection of the Institute's system, like most of the others discovered around the time of the Columbus Day virus scare, proved to be from other viruses, particularly the Jerusalem.

October 13, 1989, went off like a damp squib without the computing holocaust that some of the media headlines were predicting, resulting in an unfortunate backlash. Some felt that it had been a false alarm and downplayed the real danger computer viruses represent.

However, the Jerusalem continued its relentless march through the computing community, causing enough new infections to compensate to some extent for the failure of the Columbus Day virus to deliver full force its threat in 1989. Even now, the Columbus Day virus continues to multiply and is proving by no means a spent force. The virus activates on any day after October 12 in any year, so continue to watch out for it. The size of a program infected with the Columbus Day virus increases by 1168 bytes, followed by a slowing of the application, data loss, and a reformat of the hard disk.

Media reports claimed that the Columbus Day virus was created as a publicity stunt to promote the sales of a book about viruses, but this seems most unlikely. There was no need to create a new virus to generate public awareness. However, the speed with which details of this virus spread among hackers in both Europe and the United States indicated that there could be an organization publicizing it, perhaps the notorious Chaos Computer Club of Germany making a play for attention before a major international gathering of hackers in Amsterdam, Holland.

The *Cascade*, or *Falling Tears* virus, has now infected a significant number of corporate systems in several countries, but the actual incidence of infection is still low. It is a .COM infector that increases the size of an infected program by 1704 bytes. The visual symptoms of a Cascade infection consist of characters falling to the bottom of the screen as data is lost.

The Cascade has been around for a long time and is the basis for a number of other related viruses that may carry the same name or may be called the *1701* or the *1704* virus. The 1701 is so named because it is a memory resident virus that increases the size of any .COM files that it infects by 1701 bytes, while the 1704 behaves somewhat differently and adds 1704 bytes. To add to the naming confusion, the 1704 has also been called the *Blackjack*.

The members of this closely related family of viruses have a number of interesting features, one of which created ugly, unfounded rumors that it originated at IBM. A version of the Cascade virus looked for the IBM copyright notice on any PCs it reached and, if it failed to find this identification of a true Big Blue product, would proceed to unleash its wrath on the assumption that it had located a clone.

These viruses also employ some very sophisticated encryption techniques that help avoid detection and make disassembly very difficult. The coding complicates detection measures by randomizing the way that these viruses activate, so that no two versions are ever the same. Most only activate in the last three months of the year. Some only activate on December 1, reformatting the hard disk and destroying everything on it.

The Cascade and its derivatives continue replicating throughout the year, and when activated, behave in an increasing variety of ways as hackers fine-tune the Cascade strain. Some versions only attack certain types of color monitors: others will trigger a DOS warning message by trying repeatedly to access a write-protected disk.

The *New Zealand* soon became the most prevalent of the viruses with sociopolitical messages. It started innocuously enough by simply displaying this message on screen:

Legalize Marijuana. Your computer is now stoned.

First identified in New Zealand, this boot-sector infector acquired the nickname *Stoned* after it arrived in the United States in a more aggressive form, with the ability to infect hard disks as well as floppies and cause data loss on both.

The *Alameda* virus and its various forms have become a scourge on the nation's campuses. Student hackers have used this virus as a medium for electronic pranks or have sharpened it into a spear to tilt at authority. During its checkered history, the Alameda has acquired a number of different names (which has done little to help classify the many different mutations). These names include the *Merritt* (named after the San Francisco Bay Area college in Oakland where it was first identified), the *Yale*, the *Peking*, the *Seoul*, the *Sacramento*, the *SF*, the *500*, the *Golden Gate*, and the *Mazatlan*.

The original Alameda virus is quite innocuous and even has a built-in self-destruct mechanism. The virus only infects the boot sector of a limited number of 360K floppies, and the program contains written instructions that deliberately prevent it from infecting 80286 systems, perhaps on the assumption that those were the only systems on which serious work was being done at the time of its creation! These built-in restraints have been steadily removed in succeeding versions, and now the latest Alameda viruses carry on their infection activities indefinitely, activate immediately, and do substantial damage to hard disks as well as floppies.

Until the arrival of the Alameda, the *Lehigh* virus appeared to be the most widely spread virus among the academic community in North America. It was first discovered at Lehigh University in Bethlehem, Pennsylvania, in late 1987. Since then it has been on a coast-to-coast data destroying rampage, illustrating how rapidly and how far infection can spread through the exchange of disks among students and faculty members.

The original Lehigh virus increases the COMMAND.COM file in size by 20 bytes and changes both the date and time of the system's clock and calendar, so its presence might be spotted by an alert operator before it activated after making four further infections. The standard treatment for this most studied of all viruses is simply to delete the infected COMMAND.COM file and replace it with a copy from the original operating system disk. However, you should not rely on later hacked versions to behave so predictably.

There are a number of similarities between the Alameda and the *Brain*, another boot-sector infector that is also called the *Pakistani Brain* or the *Basit* after its creators in Lahore, Pakistan, who were the only ones ever to put their names, address, and telephone number in a copyright notice on a virus. But that was back in 1986, when viruses were not yet perceived to be a major threat that could expose their creators to retribution if caught. We knew more about the Brain's creators than any other virus writers until Robert Morris, Jr. of Cornell University admitted to creating the Internet infection that rampaged through the American academic and scientific research community in November 1988.

Basit and Amjad Alvi installed the Brain on pirated software that they sold from their Brain Computer Services shop in Lahore. Tourists could not resist the temptation of being able to purchase copies of WordPerfect and other popular proprietary software for a few bucks and so snapped up the infected disks. One pirated program can breed many others and so the Brain spread like a bushfire around the world, and was renamed the *Hard Disk Brain*, the *Clone*, the *Shoe*, and the *Houston* virus as it acquired more capabilities to infect and cause damage.

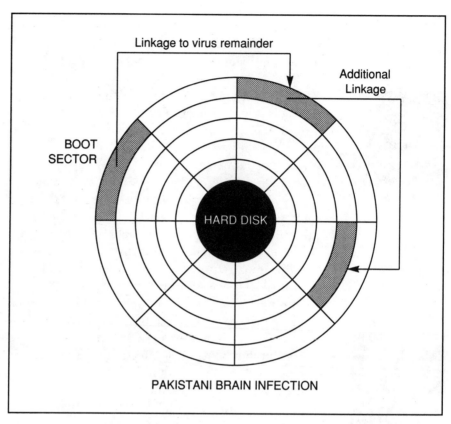

Linkage to virus remainder

Additional Linkage

BOOT SECTOR

HARD DISK

PAKISTANI BRAIN INFECTION

All versions of the Brain retain the original's clever techniques of replicating quickly whenever it finds an hospitable environment and concealing itself to avoid detection. The Brain takes immediate control of a system by infecting the boot sector on a disk, then extends that control by splitting itself up into sections of programming that are hidden in various places on the disk, which are then flagged as bad sectors so that they cannot be read by the user.

The Brain virus intercepts utilities that scan the boot sector for irregularities and steers them back to the original boot sector to ensure that the utility gets the answers it expects. This way, the utility does not probe further in search of the virus. You have witnessed the parallel situation in the B-movie scene where crooks have captured someone; when a policeman comes to the door of the apartment, the victim is pushed forward to give the appropriate answers to allay the cop's suspicions.

The Soviets don't have many PCs, so they don't have many viruses yet, but they will inevitably catch those from the West, and we may well experience more Soviet-made viruses as their own maverick hacker community grows over time. The first home-bred Russian virus seems to have been the *UNESCO* or *DOS-62*, a .COM infector that appeared at a computer summer camp sponsored by the United Nations Educational, Scientific, and Cultural Organization. It causes systems to reboot when infected programs are run.

Enormous publicity surrounded both the unleashing of the *Internet* virus that disabled over 6000 computers across the United States in 1988 and the subsequent trial of Robert J. Morris, Jr. This program was originally a worm that Morris said he created as a computer security experiment. But it contained a bug that made it replicate out of control—which by our earlier definition qualifies it as a virus, although the worm label has stuck.

The programming was sophisticated and included encryption techniques to help conceal it, illustrating that conventional encryption is not only no barrier to viruses, but can actually be exploited by them. Encryption is programming to make data incomprehensible unless you have the key to decode it. The process is irrelevant to a virus, which can just as easily destroy the encrypted data. This was the largest and certainly most damaging incident of self-replicating programming to have occurred anywhere in the world at that time. However, from a legal and historic viewpoint, the most important consequence of the Internet infection was its demonstration of the difficulty of processing computer crime through our judicial systems. Both prosecution and defense attorneys picked jurors who were not computer literate, and soon the jury, lawyers, and court officials were obviously way out of their depth in trying to cope with the complexities of computer terminology and procedures.

As Morris was being tried, thousands of medical and business people in Europe, Australia, Africa, and the United States received through the mail a floppy disk labeled "AIDS Information Introductory Diskette." The disk was sent from an office in London that was subsequently abandoned. Among those on the mailing list were people who had attended international conferences on AIDS in Sweden and Canada as well as subscribers to leading computer and business publications.

The documentation included with the disk demanded that a license fee for its use be sent to an address in Panama, and this spurred Britain's Scotland Yard to launch a blackmail and extortion investigation. The address, like everything else about this classic Trojan Horse program, proved to be a hoax. It was an expensive exercise that must have cost $100,000 or more to stage and is consequently a significant development in the history of the dissemination of destructive programming.

Ironically, the AIDS program was not a computer virus as originally suspected, but a Trojan Horse—a data destroyer disguised as beneficial software. Those who loaded the disk had their FAT scrambled and needed a utility to recover their data. Both the widespread publicity and the non-replication of the program minimized the damage. I heard of one office where a manager received the disk and threw it away in disgust, but failed to disable it. A colleague retrieved the disk from the wastebasket, ran it on the office system, and destroyed a substantial amount of important corporate data. This example underlines the importance of physically rendering useless *any* disk suspected of containing hostile programming.

Although the Japanese, Taiwanese, and Koreans now manufacture most of the world's computers, they have until recently lacked the hacker culture that creates the innovative software and maverick viruses that are found in the United States and Western Europe. The first home-grown Japanese viruses did not strike Japan until quite late in 1989, although several infections were caused by viruses that traveled to Japan by satellite telecommunications links from Europe and the United States.

≈ The Macintosh Environment

Until late 1989, comparatively few Macintosh or Apple viruses had been written, and this helped protect the Japanese from foreign infection, as Apples are very popular there. There were two reasons for the lower numbers of Macintosh virus infections: most hackers do not use Macintoshes and therefore do not concentrate on creating viruses for them, just as Amiga and other minority personal computer operating systems are not as popular as DOS in the hacking community, and there are far fewer Macintoshes in use than PCs, so the opportunities for infections to spread among Macintoshes are far more limited.

However, the situation for Macintosh users quickly deteriorated early in 1990 with a sharp increase in infections, particularly among corporate networked systems. Until that time, the most prevalent viruses outside the DOS environment were the *MacMag*, *Scores*, and *nVIR* for the Macintosh, and the *Amiga* for older Amiga systems. The nVIR is a generic application infector that has been around for a long time. It was first identified in Germany in 1987 and has since been hacked into some 30 different strains that have infected Macintoshes around the world.

One of the reasons that the nVIR was disseminated so widely and has been modified into so many different strains is that its source code—the original programming instructions—became available to hackers. The virus was one of the first to infect a popular commercial software package. When it infected a graphics program used in many companies, it gained another point of entry into the business computing environment.

Symptoms of an nVIR infection vary according to the strain. Most cause the system to crash, destroy data, and if the Mac Talk program is installed, give an audible "Don't panic" message.

The *Scores* is also a generic application infector that is very widespread—computers at NASA, in Congress, and at a number of government agencies are among those that have been infected. Its distinctive symptom, subsequently appearing in other Macintosh viruses, is a subtle modification of the icon graphics. Scores gives the Macintosh icons for the scrapbook and the notepad a dog-eared appearance.

Scores was the first demonstration of how a virus created to hit a specific target for revenge motivations can run amok and threaten the whole computing community. It seems to have been written by a disgruntled employee and was aimed exclusively at systems processing data relating to EDS, the giant Electronic Data Systems corporation. After first being discovered at EDS in late 1987, it was already rampaging out of control, attacking Macintoshes without discrimination.

The growing use of Macintoshes on corporate networks and the online activity and disk-swapping that occurs during desktop publishing activities provide greater opportunities for infection to spread. The Macintosh operating system is supposed to keep out of the user's way, and only those who are excessively curious and computer literate will venture into it. This has limited the number of viruses created for the Macintosh, but it has also put a built-in restriction on the ability of the typical Macintosh user to respond with technical proficiency when a virus strikes. Consequently, there was much corporate confusion in early 1990 when business Macintoshes started falling like tenpins as victims of the *WDEF A* and *WDEF B* viruses, which crossed the Atlantic after first being identified in Belgium.

The WDEF strain directly affects the Finder by corrupting the invisible Desktop files and causing repeated crashes when attempting to load from disk. Other system files, application programs, and data files do not appear to be affected. Holding down the Option and Command keys during a reboot clears at least the early versions of the WDEF virus.

The Macintosh world is very vulnerable to other virus strains, especially those that target the INIT resource, which performs automatic start-up functions similar to those of the AUTOEXEC.BAT files in the DOS world. Folders, Macintosh's equivalent of DOS directories, are another vulnerable area.

≈ Trends in Computer Virus Development

There has been a discernible increase in the number of international viruses being written. They are becoming more sophisticated in their coding, and consequently more effective in disseminating to find new receptive hosts, in achieving infection once inside a receptive system, and in replicating.

The Dark Avenger is a particularly significant development in its ability to attack programs designed to detect viruses, while the Zerobug is the first manifestation of a new type of concealment coding that outwits many antiviral detection programs.

The Alabama's swapping of file names is indicative of the more devious and sophisticated virus programming now appearing. Even worse was the emergence of an .EXE file infector that immediately disinfects an infected file as the user opens it. Consequently, the file appears normal, but once closed again, the virus reinfects it. The first manifestation of this technique for making a virus virtually invisible was in the *4096*, which prompted a flurry of research activity on both sides of the Atlantic. Sadly, it is indicative of the more sophisticated and more damaging viruses that will appear in the future.

CHAPTER

9

The Impact of Viruses on the Future of Computing

The widespread dissemination of self-replicating, hostile programs is having very important influences on the whole future of computing. Some of these are already apparent; others are still speculative. The harsh reality is that viruses are as powerful as legitimate software. Now our hopeful, positive expectations of what computer technology can achieve must be tempered by the knowledge that viruses and other hostile software can have equally significant negative consequences.

> *The harsh reality is that viruses are as powerful as legitimate software.*

One sure prediction is that viruses and the dangers they pose cannot be treated in as cavalier a manner in the future as they have been in the past. The entire computing community must face the reality of viruses as it becomes the norm to have suffered an attack and unusual to have had no direct contact with an infectious program. Honest appraisal of the extent of the problems that viruses pose, coupled with impartial and up-to-date advice, will be given belatedly by the specialist computer media as their writers and editors come face-to-face with what it actually feels like to be a victim and have their data destroyed.

It seems at first sight extraordinary that most of the specialist computing publications have been among the last of the media to recognize the significance of the most serious problem facing their beat. While leading computer magazines covering both the Macintosh and DOS environments were still playing down viruses, the business press, the wire services, and the newspapers have taken them far more seriously. The National Anxiety Center in New Jersey even added computer viruses to its list of the 100 things society should worry most about in the 1990s, along with AIDS, drug abuse, the greenhouse effect, and air pollution.

Apart from ignorance and being out of touch with the reality faced by end users, many computer journalists get caught up in the self-perpetuating enthusiasm of the industry they cover. Disseminating bad news or even indulging in negative thinking requires standing back from the group, challenging the opinions of one's peers, and speaking out with courage. So many computer journalists tended to downplay the importance of viruses as the problem grew during the late eighties because of the pervasive self-delusion that existed in the computer industry itself as it headed towards its first serious problems.

≈ A Brief Look at the Computing Past

To look at the future in perspective, we need to recall some developments of the near past, particularly why the virus problem was so long denied by those who should have taken a lead in tackling it.

The escalation of the virus epidemic among corporate and government systems in the late eighties coincided with a critical phase in the development of the computing industry itself, particularly in the United States. The long-term economic and technological implications meant that for the first time the industry faced the prospect of much slower growth and even serious recession in some sectors.

Potentially more important as the industry matured, the spirit of innovation on which it had thrived in the past was withering, further threatening the future. The corporate malaise that did so much damage to the auto industry in Detroit in the seventies began appearing within the big names of the Silicon Valley corporate community in the late eighties.

The industry risked losing the innovative characteristics that, in its earlier phases, had enabled small start-ups to bring exciting new products quickly to market, fanning the flames of enthusiasm all the way through from investors to consumers. Those computer entrepreneurs with the spirit of adventure that enabled firms to be founded in garages and funded by second mortgages on the homes alongside had been replaced by a generation of executives and middle managers driven mainly not by the thrill of the technology but by more materialistic concerns. Instead of bravely risking their all, many of those executives have protected themselves from danger with golden parachutes. The spirit of camaraderie and devotion to a common cause reflected in Tracy Kidder's *Soul of a New Machine* started to crumble.

The industry was no longer led by the technology's peer figures. Much of the passion went out of key companies, to be replaced by more materialistic and ego-fulfilling goals. The new leaders needed to maintain an illusion that all was well for the future, so none spoke out strongly about the need to combat the growing virus threat, which few seemed to understand anyway. The push for action was left to noncommercial interests, notably the computer science academics at universities and the end users in the business community who were increasingly suffering virus infections.

The evidence of this most important phase of the evolution of computing is readily available in the back issues of computer publications of the late eighties. This is where the interchange of information about negative as well as positive computing issues should have been concentrated. But the coverage of the important and fascinating emergence of self-replicating programs of increasing sophistication by these commercial publications, supported mainly by advertising revenue from the industry, was woefully inadequate. The real information about viruses was to be found in the fringe hacker newsletters, and in the electronic dialogues among computing's greatest enthusiasts, computer scientists, and other users of bulletin boards.

In the Information Age there emerged a schism in communications. If future historians try to reconstruct why this prevalent, deliberate sabotage of machines was so long ignored by the society put at risk, they will get completely different perspectives of the same events from among the media serving the computing community. Particularly worthy of study are the *VIRUS-L* moderated electronic mail forum for discussing computer virus issues (operated from Lehigh University), its nondigested *comp.virus* counterpart, and the National Bulletin Board Society's special virus information service. Viruses were such a major cause for concern among users that on these three bulletin boards alone, the message traffic was so high, it has never been properly archived—and so we risk losing the most important records of a significant episode in technological history.

The concerns being expressed by users fell on the deaf ears of the leaders of an industry moving away from the earlier attitudes fostering the free exchange of information and the sharing of ideas. The camaradie that drove computing forward so quickly in the sixties and seventies gave way to secrecy, suspicion, and an epidemic of litigation in the late eighties, resulting in a preoccupation with protecting intellectual property rights that put a severe brake on innovation.

"There is a growing sense of malaise, a fear that the vision and desire that once drove the industry are gone," declared *PC/Computing* in a major survey into the computer industry's doldrums.

It was left to the general media, with no vested interest in the industry, to draw public attention to the possibility of viruses creating a computer crisis. Many large organizations heavily dependent on their computers took their first steps towards protecting their data only at the instigation of senior executives who read about viruses in *The Wall Street Journal, Time,* or *Businessweek,* when the initiative should have come earlier from their in-house computer professionals. It was left to the lay media to pose such burning questions as the *Newsweek* headline in 1990 that asked "Can we trust our software? Computers are reliable, but the programs that run them are fraught with peril."

Describing software as "the invisible Achilles heel of the computer revolution," *Newsweek* and a handful of other general interest and business publications drew attention to serious public issues about computing that the industry's own trade press were failing to address:

- Software errors with the potential to cause disaster are virtually inevitable because of the large number of lines of programming (over 1 million) in a jumbo jet's computer.

- The new, highly computer-dependent national air-traffic control system is so vulnerable that the Federal Aviation Administration did not know if it could certify that it would work under all conditions.

- The software for the Star Wars Strategic Defense Initiative will probably never be fully functional.

- Nationwide breakdowns of the telephone service from software failures will be an ever-present threat.

Such concerns about the fallibility of *legitimate* software so complex that it can never be comprehensively tested were brushed aside by an already troubled computer industry trying to maintain momentum, which itself increased the risk of unreliable software controlling the machines on which we become more dependent each day.

Into this first downbeat scenario came the computer virus epidemic—potentially the worst bad news of all. The suggestion that the miracle technology might be seriously flawed was too unpalatable to be accepted at first. The computer industry was not the only sector to turn a blind eye. Too many of the management information systems and data processing professionals who had risen in the corporate hierarchy during the eighties continued to play down the significance of the virus threat, seeing it perhaps subconsciously as another challenge eroding the powerful positions their technological expertise had given them.

Many of the professionals among computer users had gained power and material success because they were not, unlike many of us, intimidated to varying degrees by computer technology. Unfortunately, for these experts, the virus epidemic coincided with the emergence of the personal computer as the true data processing power center of many an organization, not the mini or mainframe controlled by the computing professional. Ironically, if the virus problem is not contained, it could take much of the control that individual business users gained from personal computers and hand it back to the professional specialists.

≈ Will Viruses Force Us to Sacrifice Computing Flexibility?

This leads us to a distressing prediction for the future. As viruses are recognized in the business community as a serious danger to corporate interests, so the pressure will mount to curtail many computing freedoms. Inherent in many of the safe computing practices described in this book are restrictions on the use of personal computers—particularly those connected to networks or interacting with bulletin boards. This will require controls and forms of policing that are beyond the sphere of the security and human resource specialists in corporations. The computing specialists who will impose and monitor these restrictions will regain much of the power and influence they lost when data processing migrated from centralized mini and mainframe systems to desktop computers. There could be far-reaching consequences in the types of hardware and software ordered for corporate systems and in the way that systems are set up and operated in the future. Other negative trade-offs from stricter security procedures will include reductions in flexibility, ease of use, and access.

Although the level of computer literacy will continue to rise, the problems many of us experience from being uncomfortable with the technology will also increase as viruses provide tangible reasons to be intimidated by the unpredictability of computing in the future.

This new factor of unpredictability is probably the most serious cloud on the computing horizon, recalling aspects of the fear prevalent in the sixties that we were becoming too dependent on machines. This fear dwindled during the last two decades as our machines proved so capable and reliable that we eventually accepted that they are actually better at some tasks than humans and so should be given more responsibility for taking decisions and initiating actions.

> *As viruses are recognized in the business community as a serious danger to corporate interests, so the pressure will mount to curtail many computing freedoms.*

Consequently, we now entrust our lives to aircraft so sophisticated that no human being can fully understand and control their many mechanical and electronic functions. The pilot—and flight engineer, if there is one—only have limited overriding control in collecting and assessing information about the flying machine.

Many of the machines responsible for our defense and, more immediately and intimately, the life-support systems in hospital operating rooms or intensive care wards are also heavily dependent on computer control. Some of the programming for these systems is so complex that we have to rely on computers to help us create the programs, introducing greater risk of virus infection because the more complex a program, the more difficult it is to identify and deal with such infections.

This might be an acceptable state of affairs if we could continue to believe in the fundamental principle of computing that, barring understandable human errors and only occasional human misbehavior, our machines will do what they are told. However, this has long since ceased to be a certainty. There is now the possibility that virtually any system can rise up against us if it is dependent on software instructions that can be corrupted by a virus infection.

≈ Some Scenarios of the Future

Some skeptics will dismiss the scenarios that follow as science fiction, but recall that computer technology itself consistently turns fanciful fiction into practical reality. John Walker, the co-founder of the successful computer firm Autodesk, Inc., reminds us of this in his 1988 paper " Through the Looking Glass," in which he states that ". . . the history of the computer industry consists of the realization of dream after dream initially dismissed as 'only science fiction.'"

Among the prophetic science fiction works dealing with viruses and other hostile programming is the novel *Trapdoor*, written by Bernard J. O'Keefe, chairman of the high-technology company EG&G. O'Keefe gives us the plot of a virus planted by Arab terrorists that will neutralize all American nuclear armaments. Every mainframe computer in the country has to be used to try to crack the virus code.

"I wrote this parable to point out the complexity of modern technology and to demonstrate how one error, one misjudgment, or one act of sabotage could lead to actions that would annihilate civilization," O'Keefe writes in the epilogue.

We should take seriously what may seem a science fiction speculation: during the nineties, the deployment of computer viruses, whether accidental or deliberate, may have some of the following developments:

Popular brands of commercial software become the victims of industrial sabotage.

The incidence of commercial software harboring viruses is increasing at a disturbing rate. It has long been physically possible for a competitor to put a damaging virus into a rival's program without fear of discovery. Now the chances of even being suspected of such an act are reduced because the number of possible sources of infection has increased so much.

Commercial software may also be targeted by disgruntled employees, stock market manipulators, propagandists, those involved in the many copyright and patent lawsuits over software rights, and many other types of antagonists.

Some countries may eventually restrict importation of computer software from other nations that have a serious virus problem.

"We have very stringent quarantine laws which cover animals, plants, etc., but we do not have quarantine for computer software, which in some cases could be more devastating than some human or animal infections," Colin Keeble of the Australian Computer Virus Clinic told me. "My feeling now is that governments should be involved, with bureaus set up to advise PC users on how best to protect their systems."

Computer ethics will become a trendy issue, and codes of conduct and licensing schemes will be proposed and partially implemented.

These developments will have minimal impact on viruses, but will produce more tangible benefits when addressing ethical issues raised by artificial intelligence and the control of computerized information. Ethics courses, like the "Information, Society, and Man" ethics course introduced at the Polytechnic University in Brooklyn, New York, will appear in most computer science department curricula by the end of the decade.

Particularly sensitive government and public service systems will be infected by viruses at both national and state levels.

The standards of security contained in "The Orange Book—the Department of Defense Trusted Computer System Evaluation Criteria" are inadequate to protect against infections by new strains of viruses and will need to be kept continually under review. The virus creators keep evolving new tactics and weapons, creating the need for new strategies to maintain computer security. The dependence on UNIX to provide sufficient security may prove to be ill-founded as viruses exploit the chinks in the UNIX armor, particularly debugging code and trapdoors into electronic mail programs. In addition, government agencies are steadily increasing their use of DOS and Macintosh systems, which are the most exposed to viruses.

Results of the 1990 census in the United States will be questioned if there are grounds for suspecting that viruses have infected software associated with collecting and processing census statistics. There will be a strong movement to revert from electronic vote counting procedures in federal and state elections to manual vote casting and counting.

In 1988, *The New Yorker* sounded warnings about the unreliability of electronic voting, but the United States has proved less concerned so far than some other countries about the risk of what Indian opposition leader Vishwanath Pratap Singh has labeled "technological disenfranchisement." Singh warned of the many ways, in addition to viruses, that electronic vote counting can be corrupted.

"An election is a question of confidence, not just a mechanical process," he said, concerned that electronic voting could lead to the "criminalization of democracy."

Increasing fears of the future corruption of government computers will bring about stringent measures such as that taken by the Census Bureau in 1990 in asking libraries across America to destroy disks infected with the Israeli virus. That incident also pointed to an important positive trend—increased use of read-only CD-ROM disks for data storage. The *County and City Data Book* that was in CD-ROM format, and was shipped at the same time as related census material on the diskettes infected with the Israeli virus, remained usable because read-only data on CD-ROMs cannot spread infection.

A number of major infections in corporate systems will disrupt business activities in the manufacturing, service, and banking sectors.

Such attacks are statistically inevitable because so many viruses are now circulating within the business community. The most disturbing result of these future infections could be the destruction of vital backup data due to viruses remaining undetected for substantial periods. This problem will be caused by developments of the viral strains first analyzed in 1990 that infect a file to establish a base within a system, but disinfect the file every time the user calls it up so that it is temporarily normal again, thereby outwitting most conventional antiviral software.

We have already had ample warning that many corporate systems may already be infected without anyone being aware that essential corporate data is being corrupted.

"The attitude of 'it can't happen to me' doesn't work; it may already have," warned Nobel laureate and data security expert Dr. Mel Schwartz in 1988. "Just as the first people to recognize the value of the computer in business were its executives and managers, so must these same people be the first to adequately safeguard against unauthorized accesses into their data."

Writing in the *San Francisco Chronicle*, Dr. Schwartz declared that "the consequences of doing nothing at all are becoming more and more evident."

Unfortunately, it will take a succession of serious virus infections among Fortune 500 companies before that kind of warning is heeded throughout the business community, even to the extent of tightening up the current woefully inadequate password procedures that the telephone hackers of a decade ago knew how to crack with very little effort.

Particularly attractive business targets for virus attack are banking systems controlling data on customer accounts and electronic fund transfers; stock market and foreign exchange systems; and computers operated by chemical and oil companies.

Public attitudes about computers will change.

If *Time* magazine were to repeat in 1991 a survey it ran two decades earlier in conjunction with the American Federation of Information Processing Societies on public attitudes toward computers, one might find a complete reversal of public opinion on a number of key issues. The belief that computers can "disobey" the human instructions given to them and that they represent a real threat to individual privacy could replace the notion that computers are merely "dumb" machines created to do whatever we wish.

At the start of the decade, there is already ample evidence that public attitudes towards computers are changing. In her book *Aids and Its Metaphors*, Susan Sontag says that computer viruses are evoking our primal fears, undermining our faith in the information revolution just as AIDS creates visions of plagues that modern medical society cannot control.

"Now computers are being talked about as though they were organisms subject to disease," wrote John Markoff in *The New York Times*. " This shift in thinking throws certain issues into sharp relief: How much can we depend on our information processing systems? How free do we want the flow of information to be? Most important, computer viruses force us to confront the possibility that we are making systems that may ultimately defy our ability to control them."

Both companies and government agencies will continue to lie about their vulnerability to viruses and refuse to admit they have suffered infections.

Concealing virus infections because of the fear of adverse publicity has been a problem throughout the virus epidemic, and it shows no sign of abating. A survey of 500 computer users in Britain in 1989, including employees of banks and large corporations, revealed that over 20 percent had experienced an infection. Paul Duffy, managing director of Britain's Computer Protection Services, the organization that carried out the survey, said this was a conservative result because many victims were unaware that their systems had been penetrated by viruses, even if they were prepared to admit it. The Computer Virus Industry Association estimates that only a very small proportion of corporate infections in the United States are ever revealed. We may need to compel victims to reveal infections of their systems, just as we have laws requiring the reporting of pollution incidents and product defects to warn others who might be affected and need to take precautions.

Concealment distorts the seriousness of the risk posed by viruses, with banks particularly prone to deny that infections have hit their systems because this will undermine public confidence in a banking system now almost entirely dependent on electronic data processing. The consequences of software failure for financial institutions can be enormously expensive and increasingly difficult to conceal. Bankers recall the $5 million just in interest that the Bank of New York had to pay on $24 billion it borrowed to cover accounts affected by a software bug. The cost and time taken to recover from a serious virus infection could be far worse.

As infections of business systems increase, so will the likelihood of virus infections being the subject of civil lawsuits. They may, for example, be used by both plaintiffs and defendants to support their cases in liability actions. Could a hospital or an equipment manufacturer raise a successful defense on the grounds that treatment that killed a patient resulted from a computer virus malfunction beyond their control? Would they be liable if they failed adequately to protect the system from being penetrated by a virus program?

Some important legal precedents will be set in the next decade.

The Computer Virus Eradication Act of 1989 and the Computer Fraud and Abuse Act of 1986 will probably prove inadequate because the rapidly evolving computer virus epidemic keeps producing new problems. The call will be for legislation that will reach further and have more powerful teeth. But such legislation risks impacting both on civil liberties and on our ability to make maximum use of computer technology.

The numbers of maverick hackers will increase and they will become more active in creating and spreading virus programs.

This appears an inevitable trend. The copycat phenomenon alone is spreading interest in viruses among the young in schools and colleges. A generation is emerging with greater access to computers and more knowledge about using them. At the same time, strong social trends are stimulating sentiment against the political and corporate establishments as was the case in the sixties. Viruses are an almost ideal weapon for protest against authority and big business.

Even the toys of the eighties may prove to have contributed in the nineties to the increase of maverick hackers using viruses as offensive weapons. Professor Gary T. Marx, a sociology professor at MIT, warned in the *New York Times* that the popularity of such toys as those used for electronic surveillance can "sow the seeds of an amoral and suspicious adulthood."

"There are parallels to computer hackers," warned Professor Marx. "How many of the growing number of young computer criminals have simply carried over into their adult life a juvenile game view of computer hacking, in which morality is irrelevant and all that matters is the technical challenge."

Professor Marx draws our attention to the warning from Sinclair Lewis in his novel *It Can't Happen Here* that, if liberty ever were undermined in the United States, it would be from within and would occur gradually. The subculture of maverick hacking, given the immense destructive power of virus programming, lends force to Lewis's warning.

Hackers are a key element in any forecasting of the future consequences of computer viruses, and they are a complex subject. If you want to understand the virus threat to your organization or to your own personal computer, then you need to understand hackers also.

Much nonsense is being written about hackers, and if the popular perception persists that they are entirely—or even predominantly—a negative factor, then we risk losing the forces of innovation that are essential to driving technology forward. In fact, if virus infection is to be brought under control, the solutions will probably come from within the hacker community.

As Dr. Sherry Turkle wrote in her classic *The Second Self, Computers and the Human Spirit*, an understanding of hackers can only come from close examination of them as individuals and as part of a culture that expresses and supports the psychological needs they bring to their relationship with computers.

"They are caught up in an intense need to master—to master perfectly—their medium," she says. "They are like the virtuoso pianist or the sculptor possessed by his or her materials. Hackers too are 'inhabited' by their medium. They give themselves over to it and see it as the most complex, the most plastic, the most elusive and challenging of all. To win over computation is to win. Period."

Those words were written before hackers became so deeply fascinated by self-replicating programs, but viruses make Dr. Turkle's assessment even more true. Viruses will long remain among the most intellectually fascinating aspects of computation. More hackers will experiment with them, creating new and more potent strains that, by accident or intent, will be released into the computing universe.

The good news is that an increasing number of hackers will be stimulated to devise ways to defeat viruses.

One of the best demonstrations of this was the way hundreds of hackers all over the United States rallied to mobilize their collective talents to defeat the Internet worm. Already hackers have begun to organize into informal groups of electronic vigilantes, but this is a movement that could have negative as well as positive consequences if the "good" hackers deploy bug-ridden antiviral software that could prove to be as dangerous as the viruses themselves. Antiviral software, like other powerful utilities, can be very damaging to data if it contains bugs or is used incorrectly.

Viruses will be used for extortion and blackmail.

Extortion is already an established feature of computer crime. Britain's Computer Industry Research Unit has uncovered evidence that making payments and offering amnesties to computer criminals is a widespread business practice. Scotland Yard has warned that giving in to this brand of extortion could open company executives to charges of perverting the course of justice.

There is a development occuring that will limit the readiness of companies in the future to capitulate to extortion or blackmail. To stand any chance of getting meaningful insurance coverage, companies must reveal all previous breaches of their computer security. For example, a Llcyd's policy that specifically covers viruses is rendered void if such breaches are not revealed.

This will cause a great deal of embarrassment to the many companies in both Europe and the United States that have either had their systems compromised by criminals or hackers, or who have failed simulated attacks by "Tiger Teams." When the City of London police staged their Comcheck computer security exercise to test the vulnerability of business systems, some firms had to purchase software to protect their systems and create defenses before they could even take part in the exercise. Others could not tell whether or not hackers had penetrated their systems, and if they did know their security had been breached, they had no way of preventing it from happening again. A British hacker told me of the all-expenses-paid holiday he enjoyed in the United States at the invitation of a leading defense research establishment. The only way they had of finding out how he had broken into their system was to ask him to show them. "But I didn't explain how I might do it next time," he commented to me.

The future of shareware and public domain software will be threatened both by actual virus infections and excessive fear about them.

This is a most unfortunate prospect, because shareware and public domain software make some of the best programming available to the greatest number of users at the least possible cost. Already there are periodic sharp declines in the use of shareware programs because they have been associated with the spread of viruses. This trend will only be controlled if the operators of the bulletin boards and the agencies that distribute shareware and public domain software on disks take greater antiviral precautions.

On the other side of the coin, the faster pace of virus creation and release will make antiviral shareware programs the most effective defensive weapons. The bulletin boards represent the fastest way that antiviral software can be continually updated and made readily available to users.

The future of bulletin boards will be threatened.

Viruses will continue to be spread over bulletin boards and so the future of this rapidly expanding sector—there are over 30,000 bulletin boards in the United States alone—is at risk. However, the leading boards and national information services such as CompuServe and Genie will take increasingly elaborate measures to protect themselves against future viral infections and maintain user confidence. The small local or special interest bulletin boards will find combatting viruses so difficult that some may not be able to survive.

Viruses will be used increasingly to spread propaganda and misinformation.

Viruses have already been used to spread propaganda. An offensive program that could have been a virus or a worm infiltrated the NASA Space Physics Analysis Network and is now on the loose to propagate protests against space shuttles carrying nuclear cargoes. Neo-Nazi computer games originating in both Germany and the United States are now circulating internationally and can be made more potent propaganda media by being linked to virus programming that will extend their dissemination. The originals were crude; now they are getting more sophisticated. One digitally recreates the voice of Joseph Goebbels, the Nazi propaganda minister—who would certainly be exploiting computer viruses if he were still alive and in power!

There are a number of bulletin boards for neo-Nazi skinheads, which when coupled with the capacity to create viruses give great technological power to white supremacist and other extremist minority groups. A *PC/Computing* investigation into online bigotry and violence produced evidence that both the racist movements and their use of electronic technology are growing rapidly. The report ended with chilling information about plans to install a generation of technologically competent neo-Nazis in key military and government positions so that they "can eventually seize power through the use of technology and the power of information."

We now have the prospect of computers, and consequently the power of computer viruses, becoming widely available to political activists in Eastern Europe and the Soviet Union. Anyone with a political, religious, or other strongly held viewpoint may be tempted to use the power of viruses to spread a particular belief, even to the extent of corrupting voice and facsimile as well as data transmissions, all of which use programming vulnerable to virus attack.

However, viruses will not be used to spread commercial advertising. A virus that carries a message extolling the virtues of a particular make of computer hardware has already circulated, but the manufacturer is unlikely to have been responsible because identification with any virus is not going to enhance any firm's image.

This virus was subsequently hacked into a version containing a message intended to discredit a leading antivirus researcher, illustrating how viruses will be used increasingly to spread misinformation.

Increased publicity and public exposure to computer viruses will reduce our trust in the reliability of electronic communication and data processing.

In the academic community, the loss of trust among scholars and researchers who use networks was ranked as one of the most serious consequences of the Internet incident. In the future, academic and research networks can no longer be set up with minimal security so that they are as flexible and easy to use as possible. Reliance on trust among a group of users as a substitute for formal security procedures is no longer possible with computer viruses so prevalent.

This loss of trust is very significant because readily accessible national networks have played a vital role in fostering communications between scientists in the United States. If they lose trust in these networks and do not use them extensively, this could directly result in the slowing down of our scientific, medical, and engineering research.

Companies that have made large investments in time, resources, and money to get their people to use computers with confidence now face the difficult task of making employees conscious of the need to practice safe computing without having their essential trust in the corporate systems undermined.

Science News noted how the undermining of trust has been a particularly significant consequence in the spread of viruses among the Macintosh computing community, where users tend to have particularly trusting relationships with machines designed with friendly interfaces.

This loss of trust can affect how systems are linked and how expensive facilities, such as laser printers, are shared within organizations. We are also likely to become more inhibited in our use of computer service bureaus, such as the desktop publishing centers springing up everywhere.

Networks, the area of computing with the largest growth potential, will be inhibited to some degree by the virus threat.

As networks are a prime vehicle for the spread of viruses, business management may come to question the rush towards ever greater connectivity. Networking may be an overrated tool to increase productivity: future systems will need to be set up with greater attention paid to all aspects of security and to the way that data is managed, which can restrict some of the benefits to be gained from networking.

There will be a greater separation between data and application programs over networks. Indeed, with the increased power and flexibility of personal computers and the software that runs them, many networks would function better and be more secure if they restricted or even eliminated shared programming and confined their traffic to data only.

Another networking trend we can expect is an increase in popularity of the diskless work station to eliminate one category of infection gateways into systems.

Women will become more active in computing.

This is a real wild card in assessing the future impact of computer viruses. The hacker has become a male stereotype, and even though we are now seeing greater female participation in computing, males have been by far more passionate and adventurous in their use of the technology.

If past gender-distinctive behavior traits are indicators of the future, men will continue to dominate the creation of virus programming and the hacker culture generally. But women are rapidly emerging from jobs that involve the more mundane computing tasks. Although women are still very much in the minority among programmers and computer scientists, that situation is changing. For example, a woman led a team with strong female participation to update the world's most popular software, the Lotus 1-2-3 spreadsheet.

I suspect, though there is still no evidence to prove it, that the growing female influence in computing generally could impact specifically on the virus problem. This will be a consequence of women's influence resulting in more attention being paid to all the human issues in computing—the health risks to operators is an obvious example. Viruses, as we have seen, are more of a human problem than a technological one and we can only benefit as computing becomes less an area of male mystique.

The growing influence of women in so many areas previously dominated by men has opened new perspectives on important issues. Hopefully, that influence will also help us to understand and combat the virus phenomenon. We learned a great deal very quickly about the technical aspects of viruses, but still understand very little about the human motivations involved.

The complexity of the virus phenomenon is demonstrated every day in the exchanges on bulletin boards. In March 1990, *Harper's Magazine* published the results of an electronic forum on the issue of "Is Computer Hacking a Crime?" Viruses were naturally one of the main topics. John Perry Barlow—retired cattle rancher and lyricist for the Grateful Dead—made this contribution to the debate, which indicates the wide divergence of views on computer viruses, and their social and political significance.

> *I don't wholeheartedly defend computer viruses, but one must consider their increasingly robust deterrent potential. Before it's over, the War on Drugs could easily turn into an Armageddon between those who love liberty and those who crave certainty, providing just the excuse the control freaks have been waiting for to rid America of all that constitutional mollycoddling called the Bill of Rights. Should that come to pass, I will want to use every available method to vex and confuse the eyes and ears of surveillance. The virus could become the necessary instrument of our freedom. At the risk of sounding like some digital posse comitatus, I say: Fear the Government That Fears Your Computer.*

CHAPTER

10

When Viruses Strike, or the Earth Shakes, Have a Disaster Plan Ready to Roll

After the earth shook in Northern California on October 17, 1989, thousands of businesses and individuals learned a number of fundamental truths about computing. Those lessons can be a great help in developing a strategy to protect your data against virus infections and other threats to its welfare.

The earthquake, which rippled its way right through Silicon Valley, was the largest natural disaster experienced by both the computer industry and computer users. Certain viruses have individually done far more damage to data, but the effects have not been as obvious nor as dramatic as the repercussions of the quake.

Earthquakes are more tangible than virus infections in illustrating cause and effect, so it is worth reviewing what happened during and after the quake to convince you to incorporate virus infection recovery precautions into the disaster strategy you have in place for any emergency, whether it be a lightning strike, a virus, a vengeful employee, a spilled coffee cup, or an earthquake.

There were five main lessons to be learned from the California earthquake:

1. Data is usually worth more than the hardware on which it is processed. However, not all your data is vital, and you need to evaluate the relative importance of your different types of data before finalizing a strategy to protect it.

2. The loss of either data or the ability to process it can ruin a business very quickly. Computerizing your enterprise is progress with a price—it can make you more, not less, vulnerable in an emergency.

3. Public utilities and other external services are unpredictable when you need them most. You cannot always rely on the electricity, the telephone, or other services and suppliers, and you may be forced to find your own emergency solutions.

4. The secondary consequences of a disaster can be worse than the disaster itself.

5. It pays to be creative. Imaginative, ingenius, comparatively low-tech ideas can be the most cost-effective. For example, laptops, inexpensive PC clones and older Macs, public bulletin boards, the cellular phone in your car, and even recreational boats and vehicles can be cost-effective, flexible, and practical elements of a communications and data processing disaster strategy.

These lessons do not just apply to big companies—they are as appropriate to the one-person free-lance business with an inexpensive PC as they are to a large corporation with a mainframe.

In just a few weeks I have watched my neighborhood plumber go from not knowing the difference between hardware and software to developing a very slick computerized database for his one-man business. He uses Microsoft Works for his customer records, inventory, and time management, linked to Quicken for his accounting.

For the first time he knows what his business is really all about and is using his new-found computer power to sprint towards rapid expansion. It is a classic example of how a personal computer system can be a very efficient tool in a small business. The danger, of course, is that the business becomes just as dependent on its data records as does a bank with all its vital data processed electronically.

Recognizing that dependence and consequent vulnerability is the first step in creating a disaster preparedness plan. Identifying and effectively protecting the vital data is the second step.

≈ What Is Crucial Data?

There are many horror stories from the quake and from those who have experienced virus infections that give us a whole new perspective on not only the importance of our data, but also what categories of data are truly vital to the survival of any enterprise.

Do you really know what data is the most important in your life? Suppose for a moment that there is a bomb threat and you have 30 seconds to take from your office the information you will need most if the building blows up. What will you choose? The instinctive, gut-reaction decisions made under pressure of which disk to seize or file to grab as you head for the door could be very different from the priorities selected after careful thought.

Experiences after the 1989 California earthquake demonstrated that. Many people had two "moments of truth" in making choices about their data. The first occurred when they evacuated in panic at the first shock. The second came after a more leisurely appraisal of what they needed most when they were allowed only limited access back into potentially dangerous structures. (Later in this chapter there are details of some practical methods to determine the value of your data.)

Thousands of buildings were sealed after the quake—some as a precaution until they could be inspected, others because they were so badly damaged that they were declared unsafe immediately. In the area south of San Francisco's Market Street alone, hundreds of small businesses were cut off from their records and computers for hours, days, and even weeks in some cases. For some businesses already struggling, it was a traumatic experience from which some have not recovered.

When people were allowed past the red-tagged barriers back into their offices, often it was for only a few minutes, and then only one or two people were permitted inside the affected buildings. Those put in this situation were forced to make some difficult value judgements about the most precious things in the office to retrieve. Only then could they brief the most fleet-of-foot employees to put on their running shoes and embark on the equivalent of those supermarket sweep contests in which contestants have limited time to collect free goods from the shelves.

It is not only after earthquakes that such decisions are necessary for the quick retrieval of essential records. Similar situations arise in any evacuation emergency, whether it be from fire, flood, hurricane, or terrorist threat. Data is the asset most vulnerable to loss, usually the one not properly covered by insurance, and also the least well defined in terms of intrinsic value.

THREAT	POSSIBLE CONSEQUENCES									
	PROHIBITED ACCESS	DISRUPTED POWER	RUPTURED GAS MAINS	DOWNED ELECTRICITY LINES	WATER DAMAGE	MILDEW OR MOLD DAMAGE	SMOKE DAMAGE	CHEMICAL DAMAGE	CONTAMINATION	TOTAL LOSS
EARTHQUAKE	•	•	•	•	•			•	•	•
FIRE	•	•					•	•	•	•
FLOOD	•	•		•	•	•		•	•	•
HAZARDOUS MATERIALS	•			•			•	•	•	•
HURRICANE	•	•	•	•	•	•		•	•	•
NUCLEAR ATTACK	•	•	•	•	•		•	•	•	•
POWER INTERRUPTION/SURGE	•	•								
SABOTAGE/TERRORISM	•	•	•	•			•	•	•	•
SEVERE THUNDERSTORM	•	•			•	•	•	•	•	
TORNADO	•	•	•	•	•		•	•	•	•
WINTER STORM	•	•		•						
VOLCANO ACTIVITY	•	•		•						•

Often data is lost as a secondary consequence of a disaster, not during the disaster itself. This too was true after the earthquake.

Borland International was one of many companies that lost data files after the quake because of flooding from damaged waterlines or activated sprinkler systems. Borland's workers had to move out of the building for a time, setting their computers out on the company tennis courts to dry. The company, probably the worst hit in the computer industry by the quake, recovered so quickly and so remarkably because it had a disaster preparedness plan, including backups of crucial data stored safely at another location. Such backups are as vital after the quiet, usually undramatic symptoms of a virus infection as they are when buildings collapse.

Some San Francisco companies who did not learn the lessons of the quake and still failed to back up essential data had another dramatic lesson within a few weeks when downtown offices had to be evacuated yet again after a crane collapsed and damaged adjoining buildings. The temporary closing of two office towers brought the operations of 150 businesses to a standstill. Each was allowed to send only one or two employees back into the office for between 10 and 20 minutes to grab the essentials to try to continue functioning elsewhere.

At the top of most "I must have" lists, especially for sales and professional people, were Rolodexes or address books, along with key data files, such as payroll records. Only those who had duplicate records of their essential business contacts in another place, and kept backups of their computerized data at another safe location, could afford to even think about rescuing expensive hardware.

The realization of the true value of the names and addresses of clients and business contacts has made many Northern Californians rethink their attitudes about confining such information to a single, vulnerable paper record. There are obvious advantages in computerizing this data, especially in a form allowing it to be available anywhere on a laptop, with further benefits from being able to transfer and duplicate it on the new generation of pocketable electronic organizers. (Of course, if the sophisticated pocket organizers are capable of running programs and can interface with personal computers, they are also vulnerable to virus infections. But in most circumstances, they can be a very safe and convenient means of storage for certain types of data, as long as precautions are also taken to maintain necessary confidentiality.)

Those who did have a choice of what hardware to rescue first after the quake made portable computers and their peripherals the obvious selections. By its very nature, portable equipment survived the physical rigors of the quake and its aftermath best and could most easily be set up and operated with a minimum of hassles in other temporary locations. Similarly, if a virus hits your desktop system and you have a rush job to get out, the best emergency resource may well be your laptop. You can shut down the desktop and switch to the laptop, returning to fix the virus problem in your main system later.

≈ How Will You Get Online in a Crisis?

Planning for speed of recovery is very important. Many operations need to resume functioning very quickly after a disaster. Financial and medical institutions become particularly vulnerable if out of action for just an hour or two, but these days virtually every business is seriously disrupted if it cannot function for even a day.

The biggest problem for those dependent on electricity is that after many types of emergency, there isn't any normal power. About a million people lost power after the quake, most for several hours, some for days. Some of those who had emergency generators found them either damaged, inadequate for their needs, or located in buildings that could not be used. This underlines the fundamental truth that just preserving the integrity of your data is not enough—you also need to plan to have the means to process it.

> *... just preserving the integrity of your data is not enough—you also need to plan to have the means to process it.*

The San Francisco Chronicle and Examiner is an example of a company that should have been well prepared but proved not to be. It had to fall back on a portable generator on a fire escape feeding power to a series of Macintoshes for its electronic editing. This meant that reporters and editors had to switch from their sophisticated System Integrate Incorporated publishing software to little old MacWrite and learn the older, less sophisticated technology as they coped with a stressful emergency. Even simple, instinctive computing habits required for the normal system can screw up the emergency facility: If the Chronicle's reporters put in formatting on the emergency Macs, this made it difficult to transfer the copy to a typesetting program. But the paper came out, demonstrating what can be done in an emergency using basic tools—and how much easier everything becomes if there is advance planning.

That confirms again my belief that one of the best deals in practical, transportable, backup computing power is a basic Mac that you can sometimes find at knock-down prices in swap meets or garage sales. Indeed, the Chronicle's disaster planning as a result of the 1989 earthquake experience now incorporates Macs and laptops in a more coordinated way.

Not every news organization is so exposed to natural disaster by being in an earthquake zone, but all are equally vulnerable to virus attacks against their electronic editing systems, which can have consequences that are just as bad, or worse. For example, there is at least one virus specifically aimed at word processing and electronic editing systems that adds obscenities to the names of certain right-wing politicians.

As more viruses are created to promote political viewpoints, the electronic editing systems at news organizations become increasingly vulnerable. The quickest fix when an infection emergency arises as deadlines draw near could be to switch to a basic backup system designed primarily for a physical disaster, especially if staff are trained to use it.

Another quake experience with particular relevance to computer viruses illustrates how even modest reserve facilities can prove invaluable. As the 7.1-level tremors rippled their way through Silicon Valley, the timing of the quake created the electronic equivalent of being engaged in brain surgery when the lights go out for Ari Goretsky, Technical Director of the National Bulletin Board Society, and John McAfee, Chairman of the Computer Virus Industry Association. Goretsky and McAfee were at a delicate stage of dissecting a specimen of the Dark Avenger computer virus.

It looked as if the destructive forces of nature were siding with the virus against their efforts to slow its rampage through networks. Even the scanning of an infected floppy by some virus detectors could activate the Dark Avenger, so there were a number of very anxious victims around the United States waiting for the research team in Silicon Valley to complete their investigation of the specimen's programming code and develop an antidote. As the tremors rattled the windows and shook work stations in Santa Clara, Goretsky and McAfee were dismayed to hear their disk drives falter and see their monitor screens fade to black.

"Ari grabbed the Zenith laptop and I picked up my Compaq portable and we moved straight out to my motorhome parked in the garden," McAfee told me afterwards. "We switched them on and continued disassembling the Dark Avenger and working out a fix for it with hardly any interruption. We completed the work that night, so we were able to update the ViruScan antiviral software and post it to the bulletin board immediately after the power was restored."

That RV and those portables have also been used as an electronic paramedic unit at the scene of virus infections, working independently from the infected systems in the emergency recovery of data.

Think creatively about battery power when planning disaster preparedness. You may not need emergency generators to continue computing for even extended periods when electricity is either cut off or becomes unreliable due to temporary breaks or surges that could disrupt computing and even damage hardware.

There are thousands of people who live on boats in marinas throughout the Bay Area, and while power to houses and offices on land was cut off, the boats still had their independent direct current systems, often with their own generators to keep batteries charged. So LCD screens were flickering in many cabins for extended periods, proving the value in an emergency of modems as well as computers that can run on battery power.

Setting the laptop modem to keep trying for a dial tone was the most efficient way to get in touch by telephone after the quake, despite what appeared to be a major breakdown of telecommunications services. (In fact, Pacific Bell proved well prepared and soon had service restored from its earthquake-fortified central offices in San Francisco. The real reason so many people, particularly from outside the Bay Area, could not get through was due to a remarkable surge of demand; calls increased by 400 percent as natural human reaction to the disaster was to get in touch with loved ones and business colleagues.) Priority was given to outgoing calls, which is why many could call out of San Francisco, but those from other parts of the country, or the world, found it impossible to get through when making calls into the Bay Area. Many people who gave up trying to call out because they could not get a dial tone simply gave up too soon. It could take several minutes at peak times to reach the front of the queue of callers waiting for the tone. The mechanized patience of the automatic-dialing computers enabled them to complete connections when frustrated humans failed.

Bulletin boards played a number of important roles to keep communications flowing after the quake. If your network or electronic mail facility is put out of action by a virus infection, sabotage, or a natural disaster, the boards can be valuable emergency resources. The Bay Area boards were particularly helpful for those without electricity after the quake but who had portables and modems that could run from either internal or external batteries. With their own disaster preparedness strategies in place, the bulletin boards were ready to offer a substitute route for exchanging data across town, or across the world in an emergency situation.

An example of this was the speed with which CompuServe set up an emergency Earthquake Forum for those among its over half-million members who could provide, or needed, information about the disaster. Another bulletin board, The Well in Sausalito, located almost in the shadow of the Golden Gate Bridge, also did great work, elevating the value of local conference systems into national business awareness by making the front page of *The Wall Street Journal*.

In a number of quake-affected areas where telephone lines were down, cellular phone users found themselves doubly blessed with communications links either not disrupted at all or brought back into service quickly. The most severe losses of communications were, ironically, among those who had paid the most to transmit their voices and data the most efficiently. Some private branch exchanges (PBXs) were down for days, with either no battery backup or with reserve power that lasted only a few hours. Their problems were aggravated as the electricity began to be restored piecemeal—it became too big a risk to leave expensive equipment hooked up in case their circuits were fried by a power surge.

That lesson has registered with many users who, in their planning for future possible disasters, are either switching to lines that get their power directly from the telephone service and bypass vulnerable PBXs, or are adding such lines as backups. After the quake, the sleek speaker phones loaded with status buttons on many executive desks became merely decorative plastic artifacts, while the pay phone in the street outside was functioning perfectly. So don't throw away that obsolete acoustic coupler if your disaster planning includes the need to transmit data over a pay phone.

Increased interest in cellular phones for both voice and data communications has been one result of the quake. Even if acquiring more mobile units is not justifiable, cautious companies are at least keeping records of who in an organization has cellular telephones and where they are located. The people who use cellular phones also make up a high proportion of portable computer users, and you've just seen how these can be an invaluable resource in an emergency. All MIS or data processing or security managers should know who in their organizations have this equipment and where they are located. It could well be that the salesperson out on an extended trip has a version of your data that has escaped a virus infection and, in the absence of other suitable backups, can provide a practical timesaving route to recovery.

≈ How Will You Recover Lost Data?

Also being added to emergency check lists are details of the hardware repair and data recovery services that might be needed. There was naturally heavy demand for such services after the earthquake—as there is after any major disaster or a severe localized virus epidemic—and some proved nowhere near as good as others.

A frequent problem encountered with desktop systems was that they either fell to the floor, or something heavy fell on them—ceilings and light fixtures, for example. In contrast, laptops that got shook up generally found it no worse an experience than the physical rigors of a commuter flight. The hard disks of deskbound machines may have lots of intellectual processing power, but they can be really vulnerable to serious injury in physically demanding situations. A hard disk can just as effectively get knocked out when a virus replicates through the files on it, but the damage to data may not be as extensive and can be contained more readily when floppies are the storage medium.

After the quake, some victims of hard-disk failure made the mistake of rushing to get the disk fixed without giving first priority to recovering the data on it. This happens also in many virus infections. The user assumes there has been a hardware failure because the hard disk is malfunctioning, when in fact it is the software controlling the disk that is sick. In either situation, sending the disk unit in for repair without first getting expert help to see if the data can be recovered can result in the irrevocable loss of the data, as even the diagnostic procedures used to find what fault there may be with the disk mechanism can destroy data.

Short of its environment being extensively trashed, data on a hard disk can have a high survival rate through even the most dire disaster, including virus infection. But the recovery of the data by experts who know what they are doing must take place before a technician wields a circuit tester and screwdriver, or someone with limited knowledge starts using potent antiviral or utilities software. In other words, don't do your own brain surgery unless you are very well qualified!

An organization can save a lot of money by exploiting the fact that essential backup data may well run on a reserve laptop or relatively unsophisticated backup desktop system. Your disaster preparedness strategy may not need to duplicate the sophistication of your regular system. If your computing equivalent of a Porsche breaks down, you may still be able to manage very well with the old VW Beetle until it is fixed!

With some careful planning, the essential functions of a business can be kept going on one or more comparatively unsophisticated laptops, even those without hard drives. Many individuals and organizations already have these as supplements to deskbound systems, so they are a resource that can be incorporated readily and at no additional cost into a viral infection recovery program and other emergency preparedness strategies.

"Not every current company function and activity will be essential to prompt disaster recovery," points out the Federal Emergency Management Agency (FEMA) in its "Disaster Planning Guide for Business and Industry," available from the United States Government Printing Office. "Some activities must be suspended during the recovery period, some can be eliminated completely despite possible inconvenience."

FEMA estimates that vital records (those necessary to ensure the survival of a business) constitute only a small part of a company's total records, usually no more than 2 percent. Within that 2 percent could be the organization's most important assets, such as formulas, trade secrets, work processes, summaries of debtors and creditors, and similar data essential to the organization's ability to function. Most of those information assets can be stored in an amazingly small space on 3½" diskettes that will run on most laptops. And, of course, with that core data that is truly priceless, you can painlessly create a braces-and-belt situation in which two or more backups are stored at different locations and checked for possible viral infections.

Even essential hard-copy records such as incorporation certificates, insurance policies, leasing agreements, mortgages, and the like that are not digitized text or graphics data can be scanned quickly from the paper originals into disk storage. Scanners have become so efficient and reasonably priced that they deserve to be used far more to convert precious paper into digitized duplicates.

The earthquake experience has made many aware that the really crucial records for most businesses may be duplicated and stored in a space no larger than a briefcase—with still enough room to contain the laptop to make that data available whenever it is required.

> *The earthquake experience has made many aware that the really crucial records for most businesses may be duplicated and stored in a space no larger than a briefcase . . .*

The October 1989 California earthquake also illustrated the long-term sociological and demographic changes taking place in how and where people work. These changes are having a major impact on how precious data is stored and processed. They affect both the way in which viruses are spread and the recovery procedures necessary after an infection.

As telecommuting grows and people are concentrated less in conventional centralized work locations, so an organization's data and programs are disseminated geographically over a wider area, with control—and consequently security—considerably loosened. This may greatly increase exposure to infection and complicate recovery procedures enormously.

There has never been a disaster to compare with the California earthquake of 1989 that has made so many people—or organizations—make such fundamental reappraisals of their working lifestyles. Work and commuting patterns that, before the quake, were predictable and clearly defined now are being reevaluated far more critically. Because traffic congestion in the Bay Area continues to worsen, telecommuting is now appearing more attractive and practical to more people and organizations—even among managers who have always been very skeptical about having a work force functioning largely away from central office locations.

There is now management awareness that telecommuting and disaster planning can be combined, with the laptop computer and stand-alone personal computer essential elements of both. The worker exploiting such modern technological tools as portable computers, mobile phones, fax machines, CD-ROM libraries, call forwarding, online services, video conferencing and the like can be happier, more efficient, and have built-in emergency resources when any disaster strikes a company's centralized facilities.

Already about 30 million Americans work full or part time out of their homes, and this total is increasing by about a million a year. The home office trend has been fueled so far mainly by the self-employed, but the concept is gaining momentum among larger businesses also. The experience of the California earthquake provides them with additional evidence of why this is a desirable trend with previously unsuspected benefits.

≈ How to Identify and Protect Your Vital Data

The first step in formulating a disaster preparedness plan is to identify what really is vital and then make sure that it is safe from all conceivable perils, ranking virus infections along with such other threats as earthquakes, fires, floods, hazardous materials, hurricanes, power failures or surges, sabotage or terrorism, thunderstorms with lightning, volcanic activity—even nuclear explosions.

Viruses may seem at first to be similar to nuclear explosions, as there appears to be little that you can do to reduce the damaging consequences if your defenses fail. But Boeing Aerospace, in conjunction with the Defense Nuclear Agency, conducted tests that demonstrated how industrial plant machinery of many kinds can be protected by quite simple technology against much of the damage that would be caused by some nuclear attacks. Similarly, your computer—which for many professionals is their industrial plant—can be substantially protected against viruses by just taking the trouble to implement basic low-tech procedures. The big advantage of computers is that data, unlike an industrial plant, can be duplicated readily so that even if one set is totally destroyed, a clone can take its place.

Obviously, cost-risk analysis will figure in what risks you decide to cover: The cost in time, money, and inconvenience must not be out of proportion to the risk. But first you must identify what data really is vital, unless the scale or nature of the operation requires that comprehensive protection be applied to all computerized data.

FEMA suggests a procedure for making those initial value judgements when analyzing what records are actually vital. First, form a middle management project team to analyze your company's vital record needs as explained in the following four steps (the company records manager, if there is one, is the logical leader for the team):

1. Classify company operations into their broad functional categories.

In the case of sales, for example, this will include shipping and inventory control. For the finance department, account collection, payments of creditors, and cost accounting will be functional categories.

2. Decide what role, if any, each department must play in an emergency.

Not all departments are essential in the survival and recovery period immediately following a disaster. Some can be suspended temporarily, others even eliminated providing they do not severely limit the organization's ability to restore essential aspects of its operations. Any activity that is regarded as vital by these criteria automatically helps to identify what computerized information is vital also, and so should be protected against virus infection and other threats.

3. List the minimum information that must be readily accessible during a post-disaster emergency to ensure that vital functions perform properly.

These are not necessarily the records that are familiar parts of routine business, so the planning for an emergency may require some changes in procedure. For example, cash flow can be a big problem, so to keep the money coming in you will need not just copies of the last account statement for a customer or client, but also details of subsequent purchases and payments not yet charged or credited to the account. The data on an inventory report must reflect not just what was in the warehouse at the time of the disaster, but also what is in the distribution chain and in sales agents' reports.

4. Identify what records contain all this vital information, the departments responsible for creating them, and how best to implement a strategy for protecting them.

> *Information ceases to be vital if it has been infected . . .*

A virus-free environment must now be added to the FEMA recommendations concerning security and other physical controls for off-site storage. No data should pass into vital record storage unless it has been screened for virus infection. There used to be a standard security rule that confidential information is only vital as long as it is not compromised by industrial espionage or otherwise disseminated. Now computer viruses have introduced another security maxim which is far more difficult to comply with: *Information ceases to be vital if it has been infected* upon which it either becomes useless or, if corrupted without your knowledge, potentially damaging. Unreliable information can be more harmful than the complete loss of data. Virus attacks can be more serious if they secretly alter data, not openly destroy it.

Now that viruses have entered our business lives, we need not only to protect our data against loss, but also against it being altered in such a way that it could then do us harm, for instance, by salami-slicing money out of accounts. Corrupted information does not just cease to be vital, but has the potential to be hazardous to your business health. Contaminated data disks should almost always be destroyed—that means cut up or burned, because even reformatting may not be enough to eliminate all traces of infection. There have been many instances of reinfections because corporate pack rats just could not face up to the need for the physical destruction of infected disks and later one found its way back into the system and started a new chain of virus contamination.

Files that are updated regularly pose particular problems, and the only way to be sure that the backing up is taking place in a consistent, systematic way is to use The Grandfather System. Three generations of files are protected, the oldest being the Grandfather, which is always stored off site and replaced by succeeding generations of backups, which have in turn been replaced by the latest backup of current files. There should also be antiviral procedures at each point of generation change.

If there is one single, dominant lesson to be learned from the California earthquake, it is that making backups is the most important precaution to take against computing disasters of any kind. You don't need to be based in an area vulnerable to earthquakes or other natural disasters for this to be valuable advice.

There is a need to protect programs as well as data from virus infection at any time to ensure that they are available in an emergency. This is especially so if the programs are unique or have been customized to your particular needs. Ensuring management continuity, as well as the productivity of all personnel, is what emergency preparedness planning is all about. So the assessment of what comprises vital records—both data and application programs—must take the human factors very much into account. Relate your vital records to the needs of your vital people.

≈ Don't Trust Your Virus Protection and Emergency Procedures Unless You Test Them Regularly

Every emergency preparedness strategy must be tested regularly and refined as needs and circumstances change. An antiviral data protection plan is no exception.

Ideally, your organization has already developed an organization and contingency plan for self-help in any kind of emergency, with data protection an integral part of this management responsibility. If these are not in place yet, a good start is to participate in the government-sponsored courses available to help executives develop and improve their disaster preparedness capabilities.

FEMA sponsors both one-day and one-week training courses that emphasize the all-hazard approach to risk assessment, resource management, basic disaster planning, response, recovery, and related topics. These courses are available periodically at the state level, while other similar training opportunities may be accessible through your nearest university, adult education program, or business association.

It is vital that each computer operator knows where he or she fits in to the organization's overall data protection and recovery strategy.

"Design your training so that every employee will react automatically in an emergency and so that all employees assigned emergency response tasks know their responsibilities and have acquired the skills to do the job efficiently," recommends FEMA in advice that is as appropriate for a virus infection as for an earthquake. Employees should have a thorough understanding of the entire emergency plan and how to deploy their skills—or, equally vital, to know their limits and when and whom to call for expert assistance.

The testing of your strategy will teach everyone a great deal, and you can use the programs on the disk accompanying this book to simulate a virus attack without exposing your data to actual damage. It is not necessary to infect a system to test how its defenses function, just as it is not necessary to set fire to the office to run a fire drill!

Here is a practical procedure, based on FEMA's well-tried Testing Protection Program for Vital Records, specially adapted for testing virus infections. First, define the objectives of your test. You probably need to know that vital data can be recovered with the minimum disruption after an infection has occurred and be confident that your restoration procedures minimize the risk of reinfection. So your testing must prove your ability to restore records that are

- Current

- Virus free

- Safe from other possible perils, such as natural disasters, fire, theft, and so on

- In a usable form

Approach this definition task by evaluating exactly what you need to do with your data after an emergency. For example, you may have to pay employees and suppliers promptly, so you need to know your cash position and the location of funds. You may need to quantify and deploy your assets, so your accounts-receivable data must be both current and readily accessible. You will certainly need to maintain your prime business activity, so the order entry, engineering, production, and customer accounts information necessary to resume production and sales activities must be available quickly in a form that is both current and usable. This information may be next to useless if it is a week old and in archived tape format, which you probably cannot readily access or process.

For a one-person business, the basic principles are the same, even if the details differ. If you are working on a second draft of your novel, you need access to backups of that draft, not just a duplicate of the first attempt. And if your backup hardware is your portable laptop that only takes double-density micro floppies, you don't want your backups on high-density 5¼" diskettes.

FEMA recommends that advance knowledge of tests should be restricted to as few people as possible, and that in some cases conducting tests away from the premises may be desirable in order to reduce the disruption to normal work routines. Ensure that the necessary facilities are available, for example, data processing hardware.

Make your test realistic by setting specific problems with which those participating can identify. We can all imagine what it might be like if the building catches fire, but it is also important to demonstrate that the computing facilities can become as useless from a virus infection as if they had been destroyed by fire or flood damage. A typical test problem might be to assume that a virus has infected the computers in a branch office and is believed to be spreading through the corporate network. The virus type and the extent of the infection have not been identified, but the organization's main active database resources may have been compromised and so cannot be used. What would you do?

The test should validate these areas of concern:

- The organization's ability to confine the infection

- Availability of and ready access to appropriate detection software and technological expertise

- The ability to eradicate the infection

- The ability to recover so that systems are operating normally, with the restoration of any data lost and known to be virus free as quickly as possible

- Availability of adequate resources to maintain vital data processing operations while detection and recovery proce- dures are being implemented

The challenge of the test is to show that the hardware can be made functional again and the lost data rescued if the virus program can be identified and eradicated. An important part of the test is to communicate that the data on both hard disks and other storage media may be contaminated.

Not only must the computers be made to function again, they must also be supplied with clean, current data that can enable essential tasks to continue. Can employees be paid on time? Can the sources of supply for specific products or services be obtained quickly and at the best prices? Can an insurance claim be prepared? Can engineering drawings, specifications, and bills of materials for essential products be produced? Can you generate current statements of income and expenses, assets and liabilities?

Appoint managers not participating in the test to act as judges. The judges have a key management role to play. For example, they need to be sure that data that is reconstructed from backups really is current and accurate, not outdated and unreliable. Having regular tests monitored by senior managers helps to maintain an acceptable quality in data backup procedures. However enthusiastic everybody is at the beginning, if the backup material is not brought into play and tested regularly, the operation can soon become slipshod, and deficiencies will be discovered only when a real emergency strikes.

≈ Security and Emergency Preparedness

Data is at least as vulnerable to human attack made through breaches of security as it is to fire, flood, or other disaster. The human threat is increased by viruses because they can penetrate most conventional security defenses and be as difficult to anticipate and detect as motiveless murder.

Nothing is static in any computing operation. Changes are constantly taking place, either formally introduced, as when a new operating procedure or application program is adopted, or informally absorbed as user modifications. But the security procedures for protecting and recovering data must be sacrosanct and strictly maintained, with only authorized changes introduced. This is not only to ensure that emergency procedures are not compromised, but also as a basic security precaution to protect a system from possible internal sabotage or being otherwise exposed to unauthorized access with harmful intent.

"Program changes should be fully documented, programmers involved in these changes must be clearly identified in the program documentation, and both the user department and the computer facility supervision must review and approve these changes before they are implemented," FEMA emphasizes. "Programmers must not be permitted on their own initiative to make even minor changes in the production programs they are running."

If security is a real concern, FEMA recommends a number of further actions. These include assigning computer operators to work in pairs at all times, even on weekends and holidays, especially when vital records are being processed. A suggested routine is for a supervisor or senior operator to be paired with a less experienced person or one new to the organization. The team or partner concept has a double benefit—it reduces the risk of errors or unauthorized data alteration going undetected and also generally helps to maintain quality.

Loyal employees are the best watchdogs. There was a case in Texas in which a dismissed employee working out his notice was observed by another employee at a terminal outside normal office hours. This observation prompted an investigation that prevented the worm program the dismissed man had planted from doing massive destruction to vital records.

FEMA recommends two further steps to reduce the ever-present risk of files being destroyed through operator error or by malicious intent. These tips are also antiviral precautions worth taking. First, you place the operating or executive supervisory program in read-only memory (ROM). This safeguards the program's memory protection features, preventing accidental file segment destruction and blocking illegal use of the file. The second step is to include intensive job completion checks in every program to ensure that operators do not terminate or leave any program until a satisfactory end-of-job message has been logged. This final checking procedure could include running a virus detection program or a checksum, or some other action that might detect virus activity.

"Computer operator team assignments and work shifts should be rotated periodically," says FEMA. "An operator should not process the same programmer's programs for an extended period of time. Encourage operators to remain alert to facility physical condition changes. They should check periodically during each shift for such things as magnets, screwdrivers, files, and other small, potential sabotage tools; disengaged security and fire alarm equipment, and open doors to operational disk units and other peripheral equipment."

Careful scheduling of computer time ensures more efficient use of the facility's capacity and makes it easier to spot unauthorized use of computer time to copy vital information files (or to create or introduce viruses or other data threatening programs). Varying the schedule for processing particularly sensitive vital records is a sensible security precaution—do not run the program at the same time every day, or on the same day each week. Similarly, your tests or emergency drills should not follow a predictable pattern.

Protecting the data in its computerized form is effective against viruses, but it is not enough to prevent industrial espionage or guard information that might enable a saboteur to gain access to the system to plant a virus. I spoke to a detective investigating a case in which foreign agents have been operating drug rings inside at least two leading American high technology companies, swapping cocaine for vital secret data. These investigations also revealed that the garbage of companies targeted for industrial espionage was being searched regularly. It may be easier to get the needed confidential information from continuous-form carbon paper, impact printer ribbons, or other hard-copy formats discarded in the dumpster than to electronically break into a system.

Electronic media that appear to be clear of either infection or vital data may well not be. FEMA recommends writing streams of random digits over disks and tapes that have contained vital information before they are released for reuse with other files and programs. This can be good advice also for disinfecting after a virus infection. The military has been overwriting infected hard disks with zeroes as a precautionary technique, even when virus detectors have indicated that the infecting program has been completely removed. It may seem like paranoia, but the military takes viruses so seriously that it often junks hard disks that have been infected. Those of us with tighter budgets than the Pentagon cannot afford to do that, but certainly floppy disks that have contained vital information or have been infected should be destroyed. It is the only sensible and cost-effective thing to do.

The antisabotage or contra-espionage techniques recommended for preventing unauthorized access to data transmissions, for example, via line taps, can help to reduce the exposure to virus infection, but will not eliminate it. Remember John McAfee's constantly repeated warning that "viruses enter systems in friendly hands." Conventional security is not enough. Think of this situation as parallel to the lengths that airlines now have to go to on some flights to ensure that terrorists do not get on board and that innocent passengers do not inadvertently act as the delivery mechanisms for bombs planted in their luggage when they were not looking.

FEMA also advises maintaining logs of data processing activity as a means of helping to assure information integrity. I have a simplified model of such logs at the end of Chapter 5, but on the bigger systems the supervisor or the operating system program itself should maintain a log that the ordinary operators on the system cannot access. This log creates a database record of programs processed, files used, the operators active on the system, and other relevant factors, linked to time and date. Recording elapsed time for computing activity can help to identify unauthorized use.

"Computer facility supervisors and company security officers should review the log jointly at least once weekly and investigate questionable inquiries and apparent irregularities," FEMA advises.

"Computer programs used to process vital information should be fully documented. A current copy of this documentation should be stored off-site with the dispersed file-copy tape. Programs purchased or leased from another company should receive protection equal to that given to company-developed programs."

Programs from outside sources may have been adapted in some way to the company's specific data processing needs. Documentation incorporating all the necessary features for such an adapted program may be difficult or impossible to obtain from the supplier on short notice. Company computer facility operating policies will determine full documentation file content, but the program segment of it should include at least the following:

- Plain narrative description of what the program does
- Definition of transaction content
- Block or program logic diagrams
- Decision tables
- Source coding

- Assembly listing

- A register of checkpoints, error messages, and interruptions, together with restart and recovery instructions

- A description of input, output, and transaction processing controls

There are many threats to the integrity of data, and awareness of the danger from viruses merely points out our vulnerability to these other hazards to which vital records may be exposed.

≈ How Will You Keep Communications Flowing?

All the internal communications media that may have been used for training employees in safe computing techniques can be deployed to inform everyone about disaster recovery plans. This is also good internal PR, providing reassurance to the organization's computer users.

But remember in your disaster preparedness planning that a virus infection could disable your computerized communications, so ensure that emergency telephone numbers for voice communications are readily available wherever they might be needed.

A telephone help line—with the number permanently displayed at every terminal—is probably the most cost-effective way to give 24-hour support to all of an organization's computer users, wherever they are located. The information contained in Chapter 6 provides the basis for scripting such an emergency service to advise on diagnosing virus infections, and also giving emergency access to support when salvaging data in an emergency. A hot line can be either live or pre-recorded and tailor-made to a particular organization or location, or to a shared service.

You can buy a complete virus advice service, and update it regularly on a turnkey basis, from the International Computer Virus Institute (ICVI). Check also with the Computer Virus Industry Association to see if any of their members have introduced this or other new services. Consultants will probably start to offer something similar also, but make sure it is regularly updated. Old virus advice is as useless as yesterday's news; in journalistic terms this is a fast-breaking, running story in which all computer users are participants.

The ICVI also supplies the design and script for customizing an in-house hot line to fit individual corporate requirements. For example, some companies may wish to incorporate into a virus hot line service a user support service for application programs such as word processing or databases. This can be particularly appropriate when staff changes frequently, or when a program upgrade occurs and there is an additional training requirement.

Printed information detailing emergency procedures should be located at every terminal in addition or as an alternative to a hot line. You need to ensure that everybody in the organization will react in a coordinated, predictable way when any data processing emergency arises. A modest investment in such communications aids that give instructions on what to do in a disaster can be repaid many times over.

The temptation for both individuals and organizations after adopting a comprehensive and coordinated policy to defend their systems against virus infection is to not go the rest of the way in acquiring the capacity to take effective action should an infection occur. A particular problem is to leave the responsibility for both prevention and disaster recovery planning to the technical computer experts because the problem is seen as a technical one, not a people management issue.

The fundamental truth about computer viruses stressed earlier applies just as much to recovery from infections and other data processing emergencies as it does to virus infection prevention: People create these damaging programs, people spread them to machines used by other people, and people can help when infections occur.

Viruses give a new perspective to disaster preparedness because, unlike most emergencies, a virus infection can remain undetected for a very long time, and the emergency may require attention long before any visible symptoms become apparent. So virus infection preparedness must be geared towards swift, effective action as soon as possible; reaction should not be delayed until the situation has deteriorated to the point that a system ceases to function and data is lost beyond recovery.

Use good detection software to enable you to do the equivalent in your data processing of putting on the brakes, pulling over to the side of the road, and cutting the engine the moment the oil pressure warning light starts to flicker. This demands emergency routines that will first identify, then contain an infection as much as possible in the early stages, particularly when systems are linked over networks.

Finally, we have to repeat the backup refrain that has been a dominant theme of this chapter. Integral to data processing disaster preparedness is your backup strategy. Like wearing a seat belt whenever you get into a vehicle, it should become second nature to the point where any computer user feels uncomfortable if frequent, efficient backing up of data is not part of the daily operating routine.

CHAPTER

11

How to Use Your Antiviral Software

The antiviral software that accompanies this book is a special version of ViruScan, probably the most widely used antiviral program and the best proven method so far developed to combat major virus infection when used in conjunction with the safe computing practices outlined in this book.

Thousands of computer users have downloaded various versions of ViruScan from the CVIA bulletin board and used them to check their systems and protect their data from the virus epidemic. Many companies have tested ViruScan exhaustively to prove its efficiency at detecting and dealing with the majority of viral strains causing infections in the United States, Europe, Japan, and other parts of the world. These companies, together with government departments and other organizations, have taken out site licenses for the professional version of this unique software, some with over 10,000 personal computers on vulnerable corporate networks.

≈ What Is ViruScan?

ViruScan works by searching your system for evidence of typical virus activity and, if it finds any, comparing this evidence with its database of the characteristics of viruses. It's rather like police detective work—searching for fingerprints at the scene of a crime and then comparing them with prints stored in the databases on known criminals.

The software engineering work on ViruScan was coordinated by John McAfee of Santa Clara, California, who is chairman of CVIA and probably the most quoted American expert on virus protection. Refining and keeping ViruScan up to date has become a truly international team effort directed from the CVIA offices in California's Silicon Valley, the world center for computer technology. The unique feature of ViruScan and the reason why it was selected to accompany this book is that, as a user, you can obtain these updates so easily. There are hundreds of antiviral programs on the market now, but even the best of them risk becoming obsolete rapidly as new strains of viruses are created to outwit them.

But your copy of ViruScan can be updated at any time over the telephone, if you have a modem. The National Bulletin Board Society has a special virus information service that it runs for the CVIA. When the CVIA identifies new strains of viruses, has disassembled them to find out how they work, and has developed an antidote, a modified copy of ViruScan is posted to the bulletin board that you can download. Set your modem to dial 408-988-4004 and follow the directions when you get through.

The virus information service is a fascinating place to visit electronically. It contains messages from people reporting incidents with viruses, together with really useful advice on how they have coped with their problems. By early 1990 the service had received over 4,000 messages and news items about viruses from all over the world. There are also simulations of how viruses work (similar to the ones included on the disk that accompanies this book) that you can download safely and run on your own system to give you first-hand experience of what it is like when a system becomes infected. These simulation programs can be particularly valuable for companies to use for in-house training programs.

If you have an interesting virus experience—especially if you come into contact with a new strain that computer users should be warned about—share this knowledge with others through the board. This is one of the most effective ways for all of us to maintain defenses against the growing threat from viruses. The board is also your source for technical support on ViruScan. The experts will even disassemble and provide antidotes if you send them a sample of a new virus infection.

There are actually several distinct ViruScan programs to meet a variety of needs. Your disk contains the most universally useful—the System Scanner program—to check both hard disks and floppies to determine if they have been infected by the viruses that account for over 99 percent of all reported PC infections.

Large organizations and businesses with networks use an enhanced version of ViruScan that includes this program in conjunction with two other ViruScan utilities specially developed for their needs.

Called ViruScan Professional, this version for business and other professional DOS systems also includes ScanRes, which is memory resident to protect systems from the moment they are powered up, and ScanNet, which extends ViruScan protection through networks, providing essential protection for the most vulnerable aspect of corporate computer systems.

If you have responsibility for large systems, you may want to move on to the professional ViruScan versions. Details of how to obtain the other utilities are available from the bulletin board number I gave you earlier. If you have just one personal system to protect, then ViruScan, kept up to date, is probably all you need. It monitors your system and will detect the presence of most of the major virus strains, together with many more variants of each strain. These include the Pakistani Brain, Jerusalem, Lehigh, Alameda, Columbus Day, Denzuk, Cascade, Ping Pong, New Zealand, April First, Fu Manchu, Vienna, and many others.

≈ How Do I Use ViruScan?

Before you use ViruScan, copy it to a write-protected floppy disk after booting up from an original write-protected system disk. This is not just the normal backup routine that you should now be addicted to after the number of times I have emphasized its importance! Your system may already be infected with a virus that has not yet displayed symptoms, and you do not want your original program disk to risk picking up this infection.

Insert your write-protected copy of ViruScan into drive A and type **SCAN C** (if your hard drive is designated C), or **SCAN B**, **SCAN A**, and so on to scan other drives. Immediately, ViruScan begins to check the areas and files in your system that are vulnerable to virus infection. These include the hard-disk partition table, the DOS boot sector of hard disks or floppies, and the executable files present in the system.

If a virus is found, ViruScan will display both where it is located—either the file name or the area of the system—and the name of the virus if it is identified. If many files are infected, ViruScan will list them all. If there are so many infected files that the list will not fit onto one screen, press the spacebar to display subsequent screens.

The recovery procedures to follow vary with the type of virus, so you may need to refer back to the relevant sections of this book. These are the main points to remember:

- To remove most viruses you must delete or write over the infected sectors of the disk.

- If ViruScan has picked up a program infector, you should delete these .COM and .EXE files and create replacements from your original system diskettes, which, of course, you have both stored safely and write-protected!

- The common boot- and system-sector infectors are treated in a similar way using the DOS SYS command. Usually you will be able to overwrite the boot sector and so eradicate the virus; otherwise you may have to perform a low-level reformat of the disk and then restore your data from backups.

- This backing up and reformatting procedure may also get rid of the more pernicious viruses that infect partition tables, but if possible try to use a special automatic removal utility.

Fortunately, as with medical tests, the results are usually good and there is a pleasant psychological "lift" every time ViruScan pronounces your system healthy! The scanning is a quick process, but be patient if you have a well-loaded hard disk—it takes about three minutes to examine 1,000 files.

If you have an older IBM clone and are using DOS 2.11 or an earlier version, press Ctrl-C to reset the drive each time you change the diskette being scanned. These earlier versions of DOS do not always automatically register that a diskette has been changed.

Your ViruScan program is the most comprehensive, effective antiviral software of its kind available anywhere in the world—international in both its conception and application. But the program only works if you use it! And, of course, you should keep it up to date and make sure that it is also used on any system with which your computer interacts regularly. For example, companies are increasingly adopting policies that ensure their employees have effective antiviral software running on their home computers as well as those they use at work.

The enclosed copy of ViruScan is a shareware program and is the copyrighted property of McAfee Associates. If you choose to keep and use the shareware, a registration fee of $25.00 is required. Please send your check to

McAfee Associates

4423 Cheeney St.

Santa Clara, CA 95054

ViruScan is a fully copyrighted intellectual property, so it cannot be copied for commercial purposes. Corporate users are required by federal law and other international copyright and intellectual property legislation to take out site licenses if they wish to duplicate the software and protect all their PCs. You can get details about site licenses from the Computer Virus Industry Association at 4423 Cheeney Street, Santa Clara, CA 95054 (telephone or fax: (408) 970-9727), or through the CVIA bulletin board ((408) 988-4004).

Index

Selections from The SYBEX Library

• • • • • • • • • • • • • • • • • • •

UTILITIES

The ABC's of the IBM PC (Second Edition)
Joan Lasselle/Carol Ramsay
167pp. Ref. 370-8
Hands-on experience—without technical detail—for first-time users. Step-by-step tutorials show how to use essential commands, handle disks, use applications programs, and harness the PC's special capabilities.

Mastering the Norton Utilities
Peter Dyson
373pp. Ref. 575-1
In-depth descriptions of each Norton utility make this book invaluable for beginning and experienced users alike. Each utility is described clearly with examples and the text is organized so that readers can put Norton to work right away. Version 4.5.

Mastering PC Tools Deluxe
Peter Dyson
400pp. Ref. 654-5
A complete hands-on guide to the timesaving—and "lifesaving"—utility programs in Version 5.5 of PC Tools Deluxe. Contains concise tutorials and in-depth discussion of every aspect of using PC Tools—from high speed backups, to data recovery, to using Desktop applications.

Mastering SideKick Plus
Gene Weisskopf
394pp. Ref. 558-1
Employ all of Sidekick's powerful and expanded features with this hands-on guide to the popular utility. Features include comprehensive and detailed coverage of time management, note taking, outlining, auto dialing, DOS file management, math, and copy-and-paste functions.

Up & Running with Norton Utilities
Rainer Bartel
140pp. Ref. 659-6
Get up and running in the shortest possible time in just 20 lessons or "steps." Learn to restore disks and files, use UnErase, edit your floppy disks, retrieve lost data and more. Or use the book to evaluate the software before you purchase. Through Version 4.2.

OPERATING SYSTEMS

The ABC's of DOS 4
Alan R. Miller
275pp. Ref. 583-2
This step-by-step introduction to using DOS 4 is written especially for beginners. Filled with simple examples, *The ABC's of DOS 4* covers the basics of hardware, software, disks, the system editor EDLIN, DOS commands, and more.

ABC's of MS-DOS (Second Edition)
Alan R. Miller
233pp. Ref. 493-3
This handy guide to MS-DOS is all many PC users need to manage their computer files, organize floppy and hard disks, use EDLIN, and keep their computers organized. Additional information is given about utilities like Sidekick, and there is a DOS command and program summary.

The second edition is fully updated for Version 3.3.

DOS Instant Reference
SYBEX Prompter Series
Greg Harvey/Kay Yarborough Nelson
220pp. Ref. 477-1, 4 ¾" × 8"
A complete fingertip reference for fast, easy on-line help:command summaries, syntax, usage and error messages. Organized by function—system commands, file commands, disk management, directories, batch files, I/O, networking, programming, and more. Through Version 3.3.

DOS User's Desktop Companion
SYBEX Ready Reference Series
Judd Robbins
969pp. Ref. 505-0
This comprehensive reference covers DOS commands, batch files, memory enhancements, printing, communications and more information on optimizing each user's DOS environment. Written with step-by-step instructions and plenty of examples, this volume covers all versions through 3.3.

Essential OS/2
(Second Edition)
Judd Robbins
445pp. Ref. 609-X
Written by an OS/2 expert, this is the guide to the powerful new resources of the OS/2 operating system standard edition 1.1 with presentation manager. Robbins introduces the standard edition, and details multitasking under OS/2, and the range of commands for installing, starting up, configuring, and running applications. For Version 1.1 Standard Edition.

Essential PC-DOS
(Second Edition)
Myril Clement Shaw
Susan Soltis Shaw
332pp. Ref. 413-5
An authoritative guide to PC-DOS, including version 3.2. Designed to make experts out of beginners, it explores everything from disk management to batch file programming. Includes an 85-page command summary. Through Version 3.2.

Graphics Programming
Under Windows
Brian Myers/Chris Doner
646pp. Ref. 448-8
Straightforward discussion, abundant examples, and a concise reference guide to graphics commands make this book a must for Windows programmers. Topics range from how Windows works to programming for business, animation, CAD, and desktop publishing. For Version 2.

Hard Disk Instant Reference
SYBEX Prompter Series
Judd Robbins
256pp. Ref. 587-5, 4 ¾" × 8"
Compact yet comprehensive, this pocket-sized reference presents the essential information on DOS commands used in managing directories and files, and in optimizing disk configuration. Includes a survey of third-party utility capabilities. Through DOS 4.0.

Mastering DOS
(Second Edition)
Judd Robbins
722pp. Ref. 555-7
"The most useful DOS book." This seven-part, in-depth tutorial addresses the needs of users at all levels. Topics range from running applications, to managing files and directories, configuring the system, batch file programming, and techniques for system developers. Through Version 4.

The IBM PC-DOS Handbook
(Third Edition)
Richard Allen King
359pp. Ref. 512-3
A guide to the inner workings of PC-DOS 3.2, for intermediate to advanced users and programmers of the IBM PC series. Topics include disk, screen and port control, batch files, networks, compatibility, and more. Through Version 3.3.

MS-DOS Advanced
Programming
Michael J. Young
490pp. Ref. 578-6
Practical techniques for maximizing

performance in MS-DOS software by making best use of system resources. Topics include functions, interrupts, devices, multitasking, memory residency and more, with examples in C and assembler. Through Version 3.3.

MS-DOS Handbook
(Third Edition)
Richard Allen King
362pp. Ref. 492-5
This classic has been fully expanded and revised to include the latest features of MS-DOS Version 3.3. Two reference books in one, this title has separate sections for programmer and user. Multi-DOS partitons, 3 ½-inch disk format, batch file call and return feature, and comprehensive coverage of MS-DOS commands are included. Through Version 3.3.

MS-DOS Power User's Guide,
Volume I
(Second Edition)
Jonathan Kamin
482pp. Ref. 473-9
A fully revised, expanded edition of our best-selling guide to high-performance DOS techniques and utilities—with details on Version 3.3. Configuration, I/O, directory structures, hard disks, RAM disks, batch file programming, the ANSI.SYS device driver, more. Through Version 3.3.

Programmers Guide to
the OS/2 Presentation Manager
Michael J. Young
683pp. Ref. 569-7
This is the definitive tutorial guide to writing programs for the OS/2 Presentation Manager. Young starts with basic architecture, and explores every important feature including scroll bars, keyboard and mouse interface, menus and accelerators, dialogue boxes, clipboards, multitasking, and much more.

Programmer's Guide to
Windows
(Second Edition)
David Durant/Geta Carlson/Paul Yao
704pp. Ref. 496-8

The first edition of this programmer's guide was hailed as a classic. This new edition covers Windows 2 and Windows/386 in depth. Special emphasis is given to over fifty new routines to the Windows interface, and to preparation for OS/2 Presentation Manager compatibility.

Understanding DOS 3.3
Judd Robbins
678pp. Ref. 648-0
This best selling, in-depth tutorial addresses the needs of users at all levels with many examples and hands-on exercises. Robbins discusses the fundamentals of DOS, then covers manipulating files and directories, using the DOS editor, printing, communicating, and finishes with a full section on batch files.

Understanding Hard Disk
Management on the PC
Jonathan Kamin
500pp. Ref. 561-1
This title is a key productivity tool for all hard disk users who want efficient, error-free file management and organization. Includes details on the best ways to conserve hard disk space when using several memory-guzzling programs. Through DOS 4.

Up & Running
with Your Hard Disk
Klaus M Rubsam
140pp. Ref. 666-9
A far-sighted, compact introduction to hard disk installation and basic DOS use. Perfect for PC users who want the practical essentials in the shortest possible time. In 20 basic steps, learn to choose your hard disk, work with accessories, back up data, use DOS utilities to save time, and more.

NETWORKS

The ABC's of Novell Netware
Jeff Woodward
282pp. Ref. 614-6

For users who are new to PC's or networks, this entry-level tutorial outlines each basic element and operation of Novell. The ABC's introduces computer hardware and software, DOS, network organization and security, and printing and communicating over the netware system.

Mastering Novell Netware
Cheryl C. Currid/Craig A. Gillett
500pp. Ref. 630-8
This book is a thorough guide for System Administrators to installing and operating a microcomputer network using Novell Netware. Mastering covers actually setting up a network from start to finish, design, administration, maintenance, and troubleshooting.

Networking with TOPS
Steven William Rimmer
350pp. Ref. 565-4
A hands on guide to the most popular user friendly network available. This book will walk a user through setting up the hardware and software of a variety of TOPS configurations, from simple two station networks through whole offices. It explains the realities of sharing files between PC compatibles and Macintoshes, of sharing printers and other peripherals and, most important, of the real world performance one can expect when the network is running.

COMMUNICATIONS

Mastering Crosstalk XVI
(Second Edition)
Peter W. Gofton
225pp. Ref. 642-1
Introducing the communications program Crosstalk XVI for the IBM PC. As well as providing extensive examples of command and script files for programming Crosstalk, this book includes a detailed description of how to use the program's more advanced features, such as windows, talking to mini or mainframe, customizing the keyboard and answering calls and background mode.

Mastering PROCOMM PLUS
Bob Campbell
400pp. Ref. 657-X
Learn all about communications and information retrieval as you master and use PROCOMM PLUS. Topics include choosing and using a modem; automatic dialing; using on-line services (featuring CompuServe) and more. Through Version 1.1b; also covers PROCOMM, the "shareware" version.

Mastering Serial Communications
Peter W. Gofton
289pp. Ref. 180-2
The software side of communications, with details on the IBM PC's serial programming, the XMODEM and Kermit protocols, non-ASCII data transfer, interrupt-level programming and more. Sample programs in C, assembly language and BASIC.

WORD PROCESSING

The ABC's of Microsoft Word
(Third Edition)
Alan R. Neibauer
461pp. Ref. 604-9
This is for the novice WORD user who wants to begin producing documents in the shortest time possible. Each chapter has short, easy-to-follow lessons for both keyboard and mouse, including all the basic editing, formatting and printing functions. Version 5.0.

The ABC's of WordPerfect
Alan R. Neibauer
239pp. Ref. 425-9
This basic introduction to WordPefect consists of short, step-by-step lessons—for new users who want to get going fast. Topics range from simple editing and formatting, to merging, sorting, macros, and more. Includes version 4.2

The ABC's of WordPerfect 5
Alan R. Neibauer
283pp. Ref. 504-2

This introduction explains the basics of desktop publishing with WordPerfect 5: editing, layout, formatting, printing, sorting, merging, and more. Readers are shown how to use WordPerfect 5's new features to produce great-looking reports.

Advanced Techniques in Microsoft Word (Second Edition)
Alan R. Neibauer
462pp. Ref. 615-4

This highly acclaimed guide to WORD is an excellent tutorial for intermediate to advanced users. Topics include word processing fundamentals, desktop publishing with graphics, data management, and working in a multiuser environment. For Versions 4 and 5.

Advanced Techniques in MultiMate
Chris Gilbert
275pp. Ref. 412-7

A textbook on efficient use of MultiMate for business applications, in a series of self-contained lessons on such topics as multiple columns, high-speed merging, mailing-list printing and Key Procedures.

Advanced Techniques in WordPerfect 5
Kay Yarborough Nelson
586pp. Ref. 511-5

Now updated for Version 5, this invaluable guide to the advanced features of Word-Perfect provides step-by-step instructions and practical examples covering those specialized techniques which have most perplexed users—indexing, outlining, foreign-language typing, mathematical functions, and more.

The Complete Guide to MultiMate
Carol Holcomb Dreger
208pp. Ref. 229-9

This step-by-step tutorial is also an excellent reference guide to MultiMate features and uses. Topics include search/replace, library and merge functions, repagination, document defaults and more.

Introduction to WordStar
Arthur Naiman
208pp. Ref. 134-9

This all time bestseller is an engaging first-time introduction to word processing as well as a complete guide to using WordStar—from basic editing to blocks, global searches, formatting, dot commands, SpellStar and MailMerge. Through Version 3.3.

Mastering DisplayWrite 4
Michael E. McCarthy
447pp. Ref. 510-7

Total training, reference and support for users at all levels—in plain, non-technical language. Novices will be up and running in an hour's time; everyone will gain complete word-processing and document-management skills.

Mastering MultiMate Advantage II
Charles Ackerman
407pp. Ref. 482-8

This comprehensive tutorial covers all the capabilities of MultiMate, and highlights the differences between MultiMate Advantage II and previous versions—in pathway support, sorting, math, DOS access, using dBASE III, and more. With many practical examples, and a chapter on the On-File database.

Mastering Microsoft Word on the IBM PC (Fourth Edition)
Matthew Holtz
680pp. Ref. 597-2

This comprehensive, step-by-step guide details all the new desktop publishing developments in this versatile word processor, including details on editing, formatting, printing, and laser printing. Holtz uses sample business documents to demonstrate the use of different fonts, graphics, and complex documents. Includes Fast Track speed notes. For Versions 4 and 5.

TO JOIN THE SYBEX MAILING LIST OR ORDER BOOKS
PLEASE COMPLETE THIS FORM

NAME _____   COMPANY _____

STREET _____   CITY _____

STATE _____   ZIP _____

☐ PLEASE MAIL ME MORE INFORMATION ABOUT **SYBEX** TITLES

ORDER FORM (There is no obligation to order)

PLEASE SEND ME THE FOLLOWING:

TITLE	QTY	PRICE
_____	____	____
_____	____	____
_____	____	____
_____	____	____

TOTAL BOOK ORDER _____ $_____

CUSTOMER SIGNATURE _____

SHIPPING AND HANDLING PLEASE ADD $2.00 PER BOOK VIA UPS _____

FOR OVERSEAS SURFACE ADD $5.25 PER BOOK PLUS $4.40 REGISTRATION FEE _____

FOR OVERSEAS AIRMAIL ADD $18.25 PER BOOK PLUS $4.40 REGISTRATION FEE _____

CALIFORNIA RESIDENTS PLEASE ADD APPLICABLE SALES TAX _____

TOTAL AMOUNT PAYABLE _____

☐ CHECK ENCLOSED   ☐ VISA
☐ MASTERCARD   ☐ AMERICAN EXPRESS

ACCOUNT NUMBER _____

EXPIR. DATE _____   DAYTIME PHONE _____

CHECK AREA OF COMPUTER INTEREST:

☐ BUSINESS SOFTWARE

☐ TECHNICAL PROGRAMMING

☐ OTHER: _____

THE FACTOR THAT WAS MOST IMPORTANT IN YOUR SELECTION:

☐ THE SYBEX NAME

☐ QUALITY

☐ PRICE

☐ EXTRA FEATURES

☐ COMPREHENSIVENESS

☐ CLEAR WRITING

☐ OTHER _____

OTHER COMPUTER TITLES YOU WOULD LIKE TO SEE IN PRINT:

_____

_____

OCCUPATION

☐ PROGRAMMER   ☐ TEACHER

☐ SENIOR EXECUTIVE   ☐ HOMEMAKER

☐ COMPUTER CONSULTANT   ☐ RETIRED

☐ SUPERVISOR   ☐ STUDENT

☐ MIDDLE MANAGEMENT   ☐ OTHER:

☐ ENGINEER/TECHNICAL   _____

☐ CLERICAL/SERVICE

☐ BUSINESS OWNER/SELF EMPLOYED

CHECK YOUR LEVEL OF COMPUTER USE

☐ NEW TO COMPUTERS

☐ INFREQUENT COMPUTER USER

☐ FREQUENT USER OF ONE SOFTWARE
   PACKAGE:

   NAME _____

☐ FREQUENT USER OF MANY SOFTWARE
   PACKAGES

☐ PROFESSIONAL PROGRAMMER

OTHER COMMENTS:

_____

_____

_____

_____

_____

_____

_____

PLEASE FOLD, SEAL, AND MAIL TO SYBEX

SYBEX, INC.
2021 CHALLENGER DR. #100
ALAMEDA, CALIFORNIA USA
              94501

SEAL

SYBEX Computer Books
are different.

Here is why . . .

At SYBEX, each book is designed with you in mind. Every manuscript is carefully selected and supervised by our editors, who are themselves computer experts. We publish the best authors, whose technical expertise is matched by an ability to write clearly and to communicate effectively. Programs are thoroughly tested for accuracy by our technical staff. Our computerized production department goes to great lengths to make sure that each book is well-designed.

In the pursuit of timeliness, SYBEX has achieved many publishing firsts. SYBEX was among the first to integrate personal computers used by authors and staff into the publishing process. SYBEX was the first to publish books on the CP/M operating system, microprocessor interfacing techniques, word processing, and many more topics.

Expertise in computers and dedication to the highest quality product have made SYBEX a world leader in computer book publishing. Translated into fourteen languages, SYBEX books have helped millions of people around the world to get the most from their computers. We hope we have helped you, too.

For a complete catalog of our publications:

SYBEX, Inc. 2021 Challenger Drive, #100, Alameda, CA 94501
Tel: (415) 523-8233/(800) 227-2346 Telex: 336311
Fax: (415) 523-2373

About ViruScan and Virus Simulation Suite

The enclosed diskette contains valuable programs to augment your computer virus protection plan.

ViruScan is used to scan hard disks or floppies for viral infection. If a virus is found, the name of the infected file or system area will be displayed, along with the name of the identified virus. ViruScan can identify over 30 major virus strains and numerous sub-varieties of each strain.

ViruScan lets you know whether your system has been infected, allows you to isolate infected files and to remove the virus strain. It is the most widely-used virus identification and removal program available today.

Virus Simulation Suite simulated the visual effects of some of the most common PC viruses, including Cascade, Denzuk, and Fu Manchu. Though perfectly safe to run, the program provides a realistsic visual depiction of common computer viruses. This simulation program teaches you what a virus infection looks like—before it happens.